KT-546-330

101
things to buy
before you die

101
things to buy
before you die

Maggie Davis
Charlotte Williamson

NEW HOLLAND

First published in 2006 by New Holland Publishers
London • Cape Town • Sydney • Auckland
www.newhollandpublishers.com

Garfield House, 86–88 Edgware Road, London, W2 2EA, United Kingdom
80 McKenzie Street, Cape Town, 8001, South Africa
14 Aquatic Drive, Frenchs Forest, NSW 2086, Australia
218 Lake Road, Northcote, Auckland, New Zealand

ISBN 1 84537 418 5
ISBN 978 1 84537 418 1

Although the publishers have made every effort to ensure that information contained in this book was meticulously
researched and correct at the time of going to press, they accept no responsibility for any inaccuracies, loss, injury
or inconvenience sustained by any person using this book as reference.

Publishing Manager: Jo Hemmings
Senior Editor: Julie Delf
Editor: Sarah Larter
Assistant Editor: Kate Parker
Designer: Gülen Shevki-Taylor
Production: Joan Woodroffe

Reproduction by Modern Age Repro House, Hong Kong
Printed and bound in Singapore by Kyodo Printing Co Pte Ltd

10 9 8 7 6 5 4 3 2 1

Picture credits

With special thanks to Esther Adams, Olivia Bergin, Ruth Caven and Alfred Tong.

All images of products kindly supplied by the respective companies, except for those images credited below. Additional credits for
photographers and companies are also given: t=top, b=bottom, l=left, r=right, c=centre

Front cover: Lulu Guinness bag, Lulu Guinness; Hermés Birkin bag, Rob Grieg; Cartier watch, Cartier; YSL lipstick, Rob Grieg; Manolo Blahnik
stiletto, Rob Grieg. Back cover: Bocca Marilyn Lips sofa, photo courtesy of Edra; Christian Louboutin stilettos, Rob Grieg. Front flap: Swarovski
chandelier, photographed by Andrea Ferrari; Leica MP camera, Leica. Back flap: Oliver Peoples sunglasses, Oliver Peoples.

Rob Grieg: 2, 3, 10, 16(t), 16(b), 19, 21, 26, 29, 34(t), 34(b), 35(t), 35(b), 36, 37(t), 37(bl), 37(br), 43(t), 43(b), 45(t), 45(b), 53, 57, 58, 60(l), 60(c), 60(r), 61(t), 62(t),
62(c), 62(b), 63(t), 63(b), 65, 66(t), 66(b), 67(t), 67(bl), 67(br), 68(t), 68(b), 69(t), 69(c), 69(b), 70(t), 70(b), 72, 73(l), 73(r), 74, 79(t), 79(b), 80, 87, 99, 106, 126, 127,
128, 131, 136(t), 136(b), 137, 140(t), 140(c), 140(b), 142, 144, 146(t), 146(b), 150(t), 150(c), 150(b), 151(t), 151(b), 152(t), 152(b)

Scooter, photo courtesy of Piaggio: 1, 159; Tom Dixon Ball Chandelier for Swarovski, photographed by Andrea Ferrari: 6; dresses by Roland Mouret, Lanvin,
Rochas, photo copyright © Chris Moore: 11, 27, 28(l), 28(r); Kilgour suit, photo copyright © Sean Ellis: 13; Earnest Sewn Jeans / Xavier Brunet: 22; Burberry
Raincoat, photo copyright © Mario Testino: 30; Charvet Shirts, photo rights reserved (AMC): 31; Jim Thompson silk, photo copyright © Hans Fonk: 32, 33(tl),
33(bl), 33(r); Almas Caviar, photo courtesy of Cavier House & Prunier: 41, 42; Kopi Luwak Coffee, photo copyright © 1005 Todd Dalton & Edible Ltd: 49; Gelato
© Envision/Corbis: 51; Spice © Peter Adams/Zefa/Corbis: 54; Tea, photo copyright © John Rice Photography, www.johnricephoto.com: 55; Bed, photo courtesy
of Duxiana: 77; Barcelona chair, photocourtesy of The Aram Store: 82; Arne Jacobsen 3107 Ant chair, photo courtesy of Twentytwentyone.com: 83 (tl);
Lounge Chair and Ottoman, design Charles and Ray Eames, 1956, photo: Hans Hanse: 83 (b); Chandelier Small Nest by Yves Béhar for Swarovski, photographed by
Andrea Ferrari: 84; Coffee Tables, photos courtesy of Aram: 90(t), 90(b); Global Knife Block, photo courtesy of John Lewis: 97; Amish Quilt, photo copyright ©
Lonely Planet Images / Richard I'Anson: 101; Kashgari Rug, photo courtesy of Fired Earth (www.firedearth.com): 102; Jasper Morrison Cappelini Elan sofa,
photo courtesy of SCP Ltd: 104 (t); Antonio Citterio Charles sofa, photo courtesy of B&B Italia: 104(b); Bocca Marylin Lips sofa, photo courtesy of Edra: 105;
Tablecloths, photo courtesy of Busatti: 107; Portuguese Tiles, photo courtesy of www.portugal2u.com (Oscar Amara): 109; Legendary Lesotho Diamond, photo
courtesy of Harry Winston / © Hans Gissinger 2004: 116; Gems © Royalty-free/Corbis: 117; Mikimoto Pearls, photo courtesy of Mikimoto: 120; Breitling Bentley
6.75, photo courtesy of Watches of Switzerland: 123; Madova Gloves, s.r.l by Andrea Donnini: 135; Loius Vuitton Luggage, photo copyright © Antoine Jarrier:
138 (t); Manolo Blahnik stiletto, photo courtesy of Peartree: 145; Aston Martin, photo courtesy of Aston Martin; 153, 156; Apache Skis, photo courtesy of
Snow and Rock (0845 1000 1000, www.snowandrock.com): 158; Tennis racquet courtesy of Babolat Vs: 160.

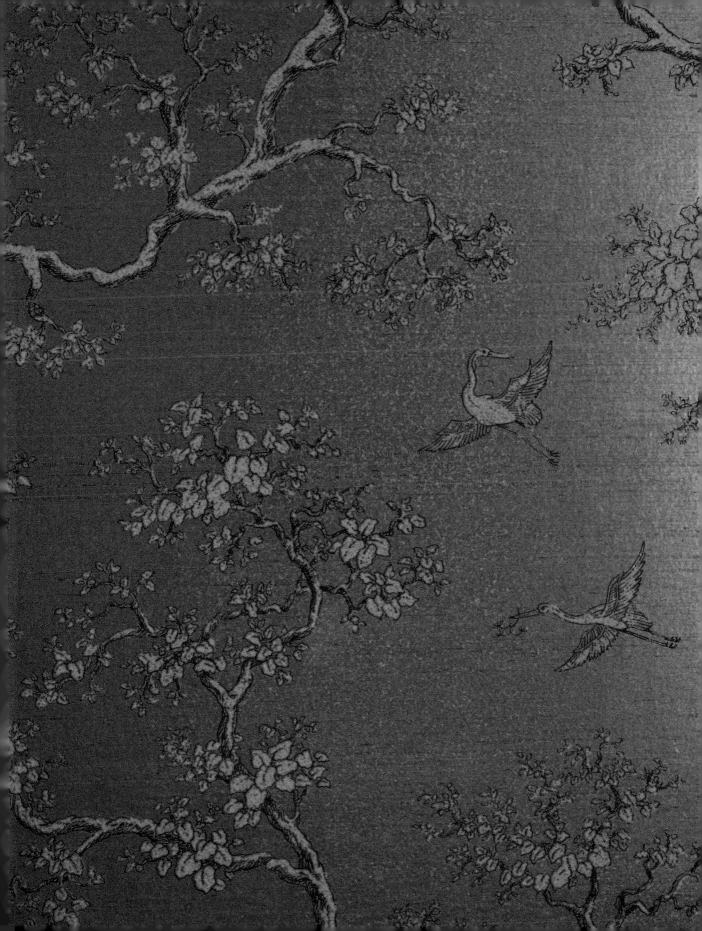

Contents

Introduction   8

Clothes   **11**
Bespoke suit   12
Bikini   14
Boxer shorts   16
Bra   17
Cashmere sweater   19
Jeans for women   22
Jeans for men   24
Knickers / Panties   26
Little black dress   27
Pyjamas   29
Raincoat   30
Shirt   31
Silk   32
Tie   34
T-shirt for men   35
T-shirt for women   36
Wedding dress   38

Food & drink   **39**
Balsamic vinegar   40
Caviar   41
Champagne   43
Chocolate   45
Claret   47
Coffee   49
Ice cream   51
Olive oil   52
Spice   54
Tea   55
Vodka   56

Health & beauty 57
Aftershave   58
Bronzer   60
Bubble bath   61
Compact   62
Face cream   63

Hairbrush   65
Lip balm   66
Mascara   68
Nail varnish   69
Perfume   70
Red lipstick   72
Soap   74

Home   **75**
Alarm clock   76
Bed   77
Bed linen   78
Blanket   79
Candle   80
Chair   82
Chandelier   84
China   85
Cigars   87
Coffee maker   88
Coffee table   90
Cutlery   91
Desk lamp   92
Fridge   93
Glasses / Crystal   94
Juicer   96
Knives   97
Oven   98
Paint   99
Piano   100
Quilt   101
Rug   102
Sofa   104
Stationery   106
Table linen   107
Teapot   108
Tiles   109
Toaster   110
Towels   111
Wallpaper   112

Jewellery   **113**
Cufflinks   114
Diamond ring   115
Gems   117
Gold   119
Pearls   120
Silver jewellery   121
Watch for men   123
Watch for women   124

**Shoes &
accessories**   **125**
Belt   126
Brogues   127
Clutch bag   129
Cowboy boots   131
Eyeglasses   132
Fountain pen   134
Gloves   135
Handbag   136
Luggage   138
Make-up bag   140
Sandals   141
Scarf   142
Slippers   143
Socks   144
Stilettos   145
Sunglasses   148
Trainers   150
Umbrella   151
Wallet   152

Leisure   **153**
Bicycle   154
Camera   155
Classic car   156
Golf driver   157
Scooter   158
Skis   159
Tennis racquet   160

Introduction

Choice, choice, choice: it's the mark of modern life. But as anyone who's stood wide-eyed and terrified on any given Saturday on their high street will know, too much choice is bewildering. Choice can be a headache.

Today, shoppers are savvier than ever before – the demand for perfection is an acknowledged element of 21st-century living – yet in most cases, although we *like* the idea of choice, what we really want is to be directed to the best: the ultimate in shoes, beds, stationery, even coffee beans. We want classics that won't lose their value; investment pieces that stand the test of time. Not fads or fly-by-night limited editions, cunning marketing ploys that encourage us to part with yet more of our hard-earned cash. It's a consumer jungle out there. So wouldn't it be nice to be taken by the hand and led directly to the ultimate in shopping?

As lifestyle journalists and enthusiastic shoppers, we're forever being asked to track down the top products available on the market. Luckily, we're also die-hard consumer junkies, the kind of girls who obsessively jot down tidbits of shopping information every time we hear them, whether it's the best paint colour for a front door, wrinkle-reducers that actually work or chocolate that's good enough to make your toes curl with happiness. Think of us as slightly younger, less manic and hopefully less ruthless versions of Eddy and Patsy in *Ab Fab* when they went ballistic upon discovering the perfect door handle in New York. We've gone bananas over *much* more trivial things... like the perfect mattress for a good night's sleep. Come to think of it, in such weary times, that's pretty crucial.

Hence this book. *101 Things to Buy Before You Die* is a collection of the very best in food, fashion, furniture and fun. Up to a point, our guide is subjective. We had one important rule: a bona fide justification for each of our choices. So we've asked specialist buyers and those in the know for their suggestions: some are spectacular and, of course, super-expensive; others surprisingly reasonable – proof that money doesn't always buy the best.

Many of the items have been selected because of their cult status; others are more about craftsmanship or heritage. Each product includes a gorgeous illustration to inspire and whet the appetite further, plus two alternatives that are often more affordable. More importantly, unlike many guides of this ilk, each choice is unbiased – in other words, no company has paid to be in this book.

Between us we've done a *lot* of shopping and much of it has been done abroad. As the Victorians demonstrated so gloriously on their Grand Tours, when they picked up bespoke marbled stationery in Florence and signature scents in Paris, a canny shopper knows it's crucial to go global to get the best deals. And, without wishing to sound too pseudy, shopping remains one of the best ways to explore other cultures – after all, local life emerges in all its forms on market day.

But if you don't have the time to source your spices in Jodphur, that's where the internet comes in. After a wonky start, internet shopping has started realizing its true potential. The result is global shopping in the comfort of our pyjamas, making the most obscure of stores as accessible as your local corner shop.

The book is divided into seven sections for easy reference: Clothes, Food & drink, Health & beauty, Home, Jewellery, Shoes & accessories, and Leisure. The prices are in Sterling, US dollars and Euros, and in most cases they are rounded off to the nearest figure. To help further, we've included invaluable advice on shopping for certain purchases – what to look for when buying a diamond, for instance, or how a good glass of champagne should taste – plus tips on haggling and etiquette in a souk. Where possible, we've nominated the most ethical of choices; come to think of it, this book is ethical in itself. We all buy far too much stuff as it is, so by selecting only the best and choosing carefully, we'll automatically consume much less.

Everyone shops. Not everyone *likes* to shop, but they need to. Yet if done properly, even the most mundane of shopping can be fun; a stick-in-the-mud retrograde man can enjoy haggling in a bazaar or browsing the gorgeous calfskin luggage at Hermès in Paris. If you know what you're looking for – and where to look – shopping becomes hassle-free, leaving you with the pleasure of owning a special item and the joy of surrounding yourself with beautiful things.

We've chosen new classics, as well as timeless and iconic cult items – all words that are often over-used in lifestyle publications. Here we've justified that overuse. You may not agree with our choices, but hopefully you'll agree with our reasoning and start buying better stuff. If nothing else, *101 Things to Buy Before You Die* should make you a more discerning shopper.

Clothes

'The finest clothing made is a person's skin, but, of course society demands something more than this.'

Mark Twain, American author, 1835–1910

Bespoke suit

Henry Poole

Where?

15 Savile Row, London, W1 • 00 44 207 734 5985 • www.henrypoole.com

How much?

From £2,400/$4,344/€3,510

There's no more grown-up, pivotal purchase a man can make than a handmade bespoke suit. The ultimate expression of power, professionalism and gentlemanliness, it is to men what the perfect little black dress is to women – a wardrobe staple that is timeless, effortless and easy. From the streets of Milan to Paris and London, Europe has a rich heritage of bespoke tailoring, but nowhere has quite the same reputation as London's Savile Row, the established home of the bespoke suit. But where do you go for the ultimate? It's tough to pinpoint the absolute best – there are now around 10 genuine bespoke tailors on Savile Row – but Henry Poole is certainly one of the most respected.

Henry Poole

The company, which celebrated its 200th anniversary in 2006, has been making bespoke suits for royalty ever since Edward VII (a renowned arbiter of taste) granted the company a royal warrant in the early 20th century. The process is thorough and meticulous: it takes at least three appointments to get the ideal suit. The tailor starts by taking your measurements to make a pattern for the body. This is finely tuned at the second fitting, where the tailor checks details, such as the distance between the back collar and the shoulders as well as the trouser break on the shoes. At the third fitting, final details and adjustments are made. The end result is slick, smart and utterly sophisticated, but also something that fits like a second skin. As Henry Poole's Managing Director, Simon Cundey, points out: 'The aim is to feel like you're not wearing a suit at all.'

Henry Poole showroom

KILGOUR

Kilgour

Where? 8 Savile Row, London, W1 • 00 44 207 734 6905 • www.8savilerow.com

How much? From £2,450/$3,583/€4,435

Founded in 1882, Kilgour, a brand that has dressed the likes of Fred Astaire, Cary Grant and, more recently, Hugh Grant and Bryan Ferry, has glided smoothly into the 21st century. In 2004, this Savile Row shop was refurbished, becoming a modern, minimalist space in which the suits hang like objets d'art, but the traditional tailoring methods remain the same. Every element of a Kilgour suit is bespoke, from cutting the cloth to the fine art of finishing. It's one of the last establishments in Savile Row that preserves the one tailor, one garment system, and it takes one of the 50 employed tailors at least 80 hours to complete a single suit.

HUNTSMAN

Where? 11 Savile Row, London, W1 • 00 44 207 734 7441 • www.h-huntsman.com

How much? From £3,657/$6,621/€5,349

Henry Huntsman established his business in 1849, specializing in breeches. The company was one of the first to receive a royal warrant, which was bestowed upon them in 1865 by the then Prince of Wales. Huntsman's bespoke suits manage to stay abreast of current fashion trends, while maintaining a heritage of fine craftsmanship.

*'**B**espoke v. Past tense and a past participle of bespeak. adj. 1. Custom-made. Said especially of clothes. 2. Making or selling custom-made clothes: a bespoke tailor.'*

And for prêt-à-porter?

Where? Dior Homme, 30, Avenue Montaigne, 75008, Paris, France • 00 33 1 40 73 53 01 • www.dior.com

How much? From £800/$1,448/€1,170

The most slick and stylish ready-to-wear suits are undoubtedly those designed by Hedi Slimane, Creative Director at Dior Homme. Karl Lagerfeld famously shed stones just to fit into one of Slimane's creations, while Mick Jagger wore Slimane-designed skin-tight, blue metallic jeans and a silver satin jacket for his last tour. Brad Pitt, Orlando Bloom and Ewan McGregor are also devout fans, and Nicole Kidman and Sarah Jessica Parker have been known to indulge in the slim cut men's trousers too. Babyshambles frontman Pete Doherty has been one of Slimane's most influential muses, with entire collections featuring angular, skinny silhouettes reminiscent of the musician's style. The suit's appeal lies in the precise cut and slim aesthetic, which splices mod and punk elements with razor-sharp tailoring skills.

ORIGINS OF SAVILE ROW

Mayfair's long association with tailoring goes back to the late 1500s, when Robert Baker set up the street's first tailoring business and named Piccadilly after the pickadil, an Elizabethan shirt collar. Savile Row grew out of Lord Burlington's kitchen garden in 1695 and was named after his wife, Dorothy Savile, but its first tenants were military officers and physicians. It wasn't until 1733, that the first evidence of bespoke tailoring was recorded in the *Daily Post* and credited to Beau Brummel, now known as patron saint of the bespoke suit. From then on, tailors began to flourish along the street, which, due to high rent and new businesses, has diminished somewhat to around 10 authentic bespoke tailors.

Bikini

Malia Mills

Where?
1031 Lexington Avenue, between 73rd and 74th Streets, New York, NY 10021 • 00 1 212 517 7485 • www.maliamills.com

How much?
Tops and bottoms, each from £60/$92/€74

It may be just two minuscule pieces of Lycra but, fashion-wise, nothing causes quite as much pleasure and pain as buying a bikini. And while colour, print and shape are all important, the key thing to get right is fit.

That's where New York designer Malia Mills comes in – her bikini tops work just like a bra, each one featuring contouring seams for shape and a perfect fit; three sets of hook fastenings at the back and three different size straps, ranging from thin for small tops to thicker ones on D-cup pluses. Then there's the all-important addition of sliders, so you can adjust the strap length on your bikini top for the right amount of support. The bottoms also come in a range of shapes, fits and styles, so you can ensure you find the perfect pair to suit your shape. Dispelling the myth that only certain styles suit certain shapes, Mills and her team take each individual as they come. In the New York store, her expert team use their trained eye to size you up, try a few things out and send you out of the door with the bikini of your dreams. 'Everyone needs to go in with the attitude that you never know what will look good,' says Mills. 'You have to try on a little of everything, because you never know what might be the surprise hit. The same goes for colour; while you might think that a really pale girl will look best in a dark brown, she might be the perfect ice princess in a pale lilac, especially if that suits her personality.'

TOMAS MAIER
Where? 1800 West Avenue, Miami Beach, FL 33139 • 00 1 888 373 0707 • www.tomasmaier.com • Department stores worldwide • www.net-a-porter.com
How much? From £155/$283/€232
Plain but sexy shapes, bold colours and modern techno-fabrics – Maier is particularly good for a fine bandeau bikini.

Malia Mills

ERES

Where? 2 Rue Tronchet, 75008, Paris, France •
00 33 1 47 42 28 82 •
www.eresparis.com •
Stores in USA, Japan and France
How much? From
£100/$175/€143
These bikinis are subtle, streamlined and constructed from a unique body-contouring stretch fabric in a range of colours with simple shapes and an excellent fit.

'You know a bikini fits just right when you feel great: you want the bottom to be nice and smooth (if the fabric is wrinkling or bunching in the back, it's too big). You should be able to really move around in your top. Lift your arms up, and make sure you don't come out of the bottom. Bend over like you're picking up a towel and make sure you don't fall out. The one thing that you want to avoid is sacrificing fit for fashion.'

Malia Mills gives her expert advice on how to find the perfect bikini

Eres

A SHORT BIOGRAPHY OF THE BIKINI

Ever since the two-piece swimsuit, named after an A-bomb testing site called Bikini Atoll, was pioneered by engineer Louis Reard and fashion designer Jacques Heim in Paris in the mid-1940s, it has been one of the most important garments a woman needs to get right. Brigitte Bardot propelled it into the public eye when she was snapped frolicking around in a cream sculpted bikini in 1957's *And God Created Woman*; then Ursula Andress furthered its profile a few years later as the mighty Honey Ryder in *Doctor No*. In the 1970s, Norma Kamali injected disco glamour and introduced the thong bottom, which became an instant hit on the beaches of Rio. The 1980s saw power swimwear as worn by the athletically toned Cindy Crawford, while a decade later, the pared-down simplicity of a neutral-toned Calvin Klein bikini was the ultimate in chic. But where does that leave us now? Well, with more choice, fabrics and designs than ever before. Today, we have extensive, attractive bikini ranges in a multitude of shapes from the string to the classic triangle, available everywhere, from high-street chains, such as H&M, Gap and Topshop, to high-end designers like Pucci, Missoni and Dolce & Gabbana.

Boxer shorts

Calvin Klein's Simply Smooth boxers

Where?
Department stores worldwide •
www.figleaves.com

How much?
£23/$41/€34

*Calvin Klein's Simply
Smooth boxers*

Compared to women, men get a raw deal when it comes to the choice of underwear on offer – it's limited, lacking in quality, and often bland as can be. Luckily, there are a few brands that have made it their mission to create simple and stylish good-quality smalls. It was 1982 when Calvin Klein first launched his now-famous boxer shorts. This prompted the trend for rap artists to reveal the waistband, making men's underwear a major fashion statement for the first time ever. Still hugely popular, the classic Calvin Klein boxer short, available simply in black, white or grey, remains the number one choice for men across the world.

J. CREW OXFORD BOXER SHORTS
Where? www.jcrew.com
How much? Two for £16/$28/€23
American company, J. Crew, does a fine selection of quality boxer shorts in varying colours and prints with no fuss. The ultimate classic is their lightweight cotton style, which is washed for softness and has an elastic waistband and fly front.

HANRO
Where? www.figleaves.com
How much? £32/$57/€47
These luxurious Swiss-made mercerized cotton boxer shorts in a classic, very simple style are comfortable and cool, and feature an all-important supportive front and soft, elasticated waistband. Sleek and stylish.

And for the best swim trunks . . .

Where? www.vilebrequin.com
How much? £75/$133/€110

While women have a thousand and one bikini brands to choose from (see pages 14–15) the choice of men's swimwear is limited and ranges from classic Speedos to tiger-print Versace – both equally awkward on the wrong physique. A much safer option is to go for classic surfer shorts. Quicksilver and Mambo are good choices for teens and twentysomethings, and Hackett offers more grown-up styles for guys. But the best quality swimming trunks can be found at Vilebrequin, which has shops in both London and St Tropez and offers six different shapes, ranging from its long Okoa style to the boxer-short shaped Malibu. They come in 80 designs from colourful modern renditions of Hawaiian prints and sea horses to classic checks. Best of all, they won't get you laughed off the beach.

Vilebrequin

Bra

Cadolle's Cara

Where?

255 Rue Saint Honoré, 75001, Paris, France • 00 33 1 42 60 94 94 • www.cadolle.com

How much?

£380/$682/€555

One simply *must* buy one's underwear in Paris, the land of lovers and the location of the world's largest lingerie department, found in Galeries Lafayette. French women understand the importance of good underwear, that it gives you confidence, makes you feel super-sexy and ready to conquer the world. And nothing is more important than a bra that fits properly – a good one should change the appearance of your entire upper body. Alice Cadolle offers a unique made-to-measure bra service. Famous clients have included the legendary double agent Mata Hari, for whom a metal bra was created, Coco Chanel, who requested a chest-flattening design, as well as Catherine Deneuve, Brigitte Bardot and Christina Onassis. The *atelier* is located at the end of a courtyard, near the Hotel Costes, and looks like a scene straight out of the classic Audrey Hepburn movie *Funny Face* – think red velvet curtains and assistants with tape measures strewn around their necks. The boutique is now

Alice Cadolle shop front in Paris

run by Poupie – her great-great grandmother was the inventor of the bra and her mother, Alice, became famous for the made-to-measure service. Poupie has retained the company's heritage, as well as its devotion to quality, and her loyal customers come from all over the world. 'The English love eccentricity while the French love tradition and good taste,' she explains. 'Americans are very boring – they just want nude.'

The Cara, an everyday bra, is Poupie's attempt to reverse the trend for round, tennis-ball breasts, spurred on by the boom in plastic surgery. 'I want to reinvent the bra and create the perfect bust,' she explains. With the Cara, the breasts point from the bottom up and the back is low for support. 'The back needs to be low so the front goes up. You need rigid seams and rigid straps. I only use elastic at the back… Seamless bras don't support – they're a killer. In ten years time, my clients will be the women who've been wearing seamless bras!'

At least two fittings are required over a six-week period, and Poupie can conjure up whatever a client desires. Silk is the least effective fabric for a bra, nylon netting the best, and Cadolle has 60 different shades to choose from and 50 different types of lace. 'Skin colour is so unsexy, but it's the most popular.' So revolutionary is the Cara, that Poupie won't let anyone photograph it for fear of copyright theft. Curious lingerie lovers should visit the shop, though, where a prototype has pride of place on an ostentatious gold mannequin.

LA PERLA

Where? La Perla stores worldwide • www.laperla.com

How much? From £26/$47/€38

The Italian luxury label is best for decorating small breasts. Think sexy lace and elegant silk fabrics – particularly their Black Label range. No wonder men make up 30 per cent of all La Perla's customers.

BRAVISSIMO

Where? Stores nationwide in the UK • www.bravissimo.com

How much? £21/$38/€31

Bravissimo is the best – nay, a godsend – for bigger busts. The company was founded by Sara Tremellen in 1995, when she became pregnant and couldn't find a bra to fit. They stock a wide range of cup sizes, from D to JJ, and their bras come in a variety of different shapes, styles and colours.

BRASSIERE BASICS

Rigby & Peller, corsetières to the Queen, are famous for their crack squad of fitters, who can tell the size of a woman's bra just by looking at her breasts. Indeed, their shop assistants are known to refuse to sell ill-fitting bras. Rigby & Peller, 22A Conduit St, London, W1, www.rigbyandpeller.com.

'*Around 75 per cent of all women are wearing the wrong size bra. Walking down the street I see so many women whose breasts hang too low – this seems the most common problem. Whatever you may have heard, it's impossible to work out your bra size at home using a tape measure. Instead, go for a professional fitting at a reputable lingerie store and try on as many different styles as possible. The perfect bra should be snug around the ribcage. If it's too big round the back, the breasts are too low; too small round the cup, you will have four bosoms instead of two; too small around the back and it will hurt. The right bra should run in one line around your body. The underwiring should lie behind the breast tissue, almost under the armpit.*

One way of checking if your bra fits is to do the finger test: place your index finger under your bra and run it round your body. If your bra starts riding up, the size is too big. Some women blame falling straps on sloping shoulders. Again, this is a sign of an ill-fitting bra. A good bra should never fall off the shoulders.

Many women's bra sizes fluctuate during the month. I recommend getting different bra sizes for different periods – if you value your breasts and don't want them to sag, this is a wise investment. Also, women should never wear wires while pregnant as their breasts are continually growing. The bra needs to be able to grow with the breast tissue – underwiring prevents this. Bras have a life of around two years and need to be handwashed. After that, throw them away!'

Jill Kenton, owner of Rigby & Peller

The Giselle range from Rigby & Peller

Rigby & Peller

Cashmere sweater

Loro Piana v-neck sweater

Where?
47 Sloane Street, London, SW1 • 00 44 207 235 3203 •
821 Madison Avenue, New York, NY 10021 • 00 1 212 980 7961 • Plus branches •
www.loropiana.com

How much?
£395/$693/€586

Loro Piana is cashmere's holy grail. According to buyers and textile snobs alike, it's the very best money can buy, and the label every aficionado worth their Ralph Lauren cable-knit (another classic) aspires to. If only it weren't so darned expensive. Yet with Loro Piana, feeling really is believing – the eyebrow-rising prices are the result of Loro Piana's stringent quality control. The company only uses the purest white cashmere, the most rare and therefore the most covetable, from the Kel goat, which is found in remote high-altitude regions of Central Asia. The higher the altitude, the finer the yarn – or so the theory goes. The Italian family firm was started in the 18th century in Trivero, an Italian centre for textiles, and it is now run by two very dapper brothers, Pier Luigi and Sergio Loro Piana. As well as its own-brand collection – the company's wraps and men's suits also come highly recommended – and bespoke service, Loro Piana is the world's largest cashmere producer and supplies fabric for labels as diverse as Jil Sander, Giorgio Armani and J. Crew.

Loro Piana v-neck sweater

Pringle

PRINGLE V-NECK SWEATER

Where? 112 New Bond Street, London, W1 •
Plus stockists • 00 44 207 297 4580 •
www.pringlescotland.com

How much? Prices from £200/$351/€297
Pringle's trademark – a rampant Scottish lion –
is recognizable throughout the world, and the
label was the one that stylish stars of the
1950s, like Grace Kelly and Lauren Bacall,
turned to for their twin sets. Founded in
1815 by Robert Pringle, the brand has
been revamped in recent years and given
a fresher, more fashionable image.

LUCIEN PELLAT-FINET SWEATER

Where? 1 Rue de Montalembert,
75007, Paris, France • 00 33 1 42 22
22 77 • www.lucienpellat-finet.com

How much? From
£1,000/$1,815/€1,477

A Lucien Pellat-Finet sweater screams
Euroluxe and is much more exciting than a
standard black roll-neck. Worth every
penny for the wow factor and top-notch
craftsmanship, these sweaters sport
psychedelic colours and nutty motifs –
think skulls, medals and marijuana leaves.

Lucien Pellat-Finet

Cheap Chinese cashmere

Where? Lin Mei Chin, 93 Ling Ling Road,
Beijing, China • 00 86 1370 195 5249

How much? A set of three should cost
around £200/$380/€360

The reason for the recent influx in cheaper
cashmere is mass-production in China,
where costs are low. Chinese cashmere has
never been good – it doesn't have the
heritage or technology – but that's swiftly
changing, although Italy and Scotland will
continue to lead the way for some time. If
you ever find yourself in Beijing, be sure to
visit Lin Mei Ching, who custom-makes
sweaters in multi-ply cashmere.

CASHMERE THAT LASTS A LIFETIME

To dry-clean or not to dry-clean, that is the question many a cashmere fan must ponder. Shyama Fernardo from the Cashmere Clinic (11 Beauchamp Place, London W1, 00 44 207 584 9806), the only place the well-heeled ladies of West London trust with their two-ply, offers some tips:

- Some people are good at washing cashmere, some people are bad – it's as simple as that. You should find out what you are – if you're bad, take your garments to a cashmere professional.
- You have to be careful and cherish your cashmere, otherwise it will be ruined. We send our clients' garments to Scotland, as their cashmere heritage means they're the best people for the job.
- I would never advise anyone to dry-clean their cashmere as the chemicals will shorten its life. Instead, wash on either a cool wash or handwash cycle using Woolite – but only a little – or a mild, baby shampoo.
- Once the cashmere has been slowly spun, gently squeeze out a little before reshaping and drying it flat on a towel.
- Handwashing is not as effective, as you need to get rid of all the water, which requires patience; if soap remains, the cashmere will be matted.
- As for the perennial problem of stretching, the only way to get cashmere back to its original size is to wash it. During the process, it will shrink.

And for the perfect pashmina?

Where? Tashia, 178 Walton Street, London, SW3 • 00 44 207 589 0082 • www.tashia.com

'The best pashminas are woven in Katmandu, Nepal. They are much better quality than the cheap machine-woven ones from India.

The perfect fabric mixture is 65 per cent cashmere and 35 per cent silk. If the fabric is too soft the shawl will start bobbling. If it has too much silk, the shawl will be too shiny. Tassels are also very important. Too thick is downright nasty and too thin is cheap looking. The Nepalese tassles are rolled by hand, rather like cigars! Taking care of your pashmina is also important. The worst thing you can do is dry-clean or machine-wash it. To keep it looking gorgeous, handwash in warm water with shampoo then roll and lay flat.'

Sara Chiaramonte of Tashia

Tashia Pashminas

Jeans for women

Earnest Cut & Sew

Where?
821 Washington Street, New York,
NY 10014 • 00 1 212 242 3414 •
www.earnestsewn.com •
Selfridges, 400 Oxford Street,
London, W1, and branches •
00 44 8708 377 377

How much?
From £150/$264/€220

What is it about jeans? They're so simple, yet so desirable; they are both everyday and the height of glamour, gliding from the office to cocktail bar with just a few accessory changes. In fact, denim is now so alluring that we live in an age when it's not unusual to part with £150 on a pair of jeans – make that £400 if you want made-to-measure. But which jeans are the most coveted of them all? Remember, like perfume and bikinis, buying jeans is a highly personal thing – different brands and shapes suit different people and it's all about trying them on. However, there are some jeans out there that are guaranteed to fulfil all desires. These are the styles and brands, for men and women, that shine above the rest in terms of quality, fit and wash.

A few years ago, New York-based Scott Morrison, former co-founder/designer of Paper Denim & Cloth, set about trying to establish the finest jeans brand in the world – the result was Earnest Cut & Sew. Fusing the garment's American workwear origins with the ancient Japanese style asthetic Wabi Sabi, the range includes high-quality denim and superior cuts. And if you're not taken with the luscious cigarette-style slim jeans, you can get your very own pair made-to-measure, a service available at the New York store, Barneys, and at Selfridges, London, where you decide which cut, buttons, rivets, thread colour and back pocket you would like. The quest for the perfect jeans might just be over.

Earnest Sewn Harlan

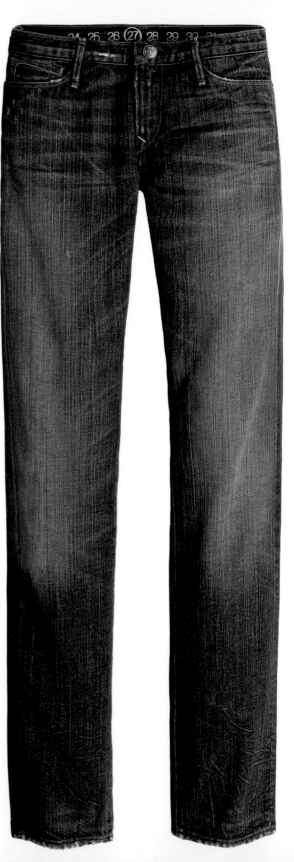

CITIZENS OF HUMANITY

Where? Selfridges (see opposite) • www.shopbop.com
How much? £175/$308/€257

Created by Jerome Dahan, formerly of Seven, Citizens of Humanity's jeans have a low-rise waistband, but not too low, and are accommodating around the hips, thighs and bottom, making the legs seem miraculously thinner. The Elle shape is a tight-fitting stretch jean in a lovely dark wash, while the Naomi is a slim-fitting bootleg that flatters most figures.

SEVEN FOR ALL MANKIND

Where? Harvey Nichols, 109–125 Knightsbridge, London, SW1 • 00 44 207 235 5000 • www.eluxury.com
How much? From £150/$264/€220

Seven For All Mankind jeans

When Seven jeans burst onto the scene in 2000, they became an instant hit, due to the remarkably slimming cut. Now, despite numerous new competitors, Seven jeans, with 'For All Mankind' added to the moniker, remain ultra-desirable thanks to the simple, flattering silhouette and deep-blue washes.

> *I wish I had invented blue jeans... Jeans are expressive and discreet, they have sex appeal and simplicity – everything I could want for the clothes I design.'*
>
> Yves Saint Laurent, fashion designer

> *Jeans are your most important piece of clothing, no question. They have to be worn. And they've got to be old. I also prefer that they be button-fly. The right jeans and a T-shirt can be sexier than the most expensive tailored suit.'*
>
> Donna Karan, fashion designer

The best...

Skinny jeans are by Acne, Notify and Superfine, they're good on lean and gamine types. Available at www.brownsfashion.co.uk.

White jeans are by James Cured by Sewn – the five pocket stretch cord rocks. Surprisingly flattering. Available at www.shopbop.com.

Cropped jeans are by Citizens of Humanity – the cropped 'Kelly' stretch is the one you're after. Available at Selfridges (see above).

All-round flattering jeans are Paige Denim's Laurel Canyon five-pocket stretch, thanks to lean styling, a permanent crease at the front and well-placed pockets. Available at Harvey Nichols (see above).

Sassy LA jeans are by Serfontaine, Blue Cult and Juicy Couture, and are excellent for curvy girls. Available at Harvey Nichols and Selfridges (see above).

Rock and roll cool jeans are by True Religion due to their slouchy fit, funky pocket stitching and distressed detailing.

Deconstructed jeans with a modern edge are by Ødyn, a relatively new Swedish brand that offers a fresh look and nice antidote to all those LA brands. Available at www.revolveclothing.com.

Jeans for men

Rogan

Rogan

Where?
www.rogannyc.com • Fred Segal, 8100 Melrose Avenue, Los Angeles, CA 90046 •
00 1 310 451 9002 • Liberty, 222 Regent Street, London, W1 • 00 44 207 734 1234
How much?
From £190/$335/€278

Rogan Gregory set up his company a few years back, with the aim of creating a denim range using top-quality yarns and washes with a social and environmental purpose. His wonderfully well-designed Original jeans are one of the sexiest, coolest and best-fitting styles men can buy, made with fine dyes, excellent tailoring and limited editions designed by Max Fenton.

PAPER DENIM & CLOTH
Where? Start, 57 Rivington Street, London, EC2 • 00 44 207 739 3636 • www.paperdenim.com
How much? From £170/$300/€249
This range, favoured by Tom Cruise, features jeans that are just the right fit – slim, but with a hint of bagginess, and good on the backside (i.e. not too low) – which makes them among the most wearable jeans out there. The recently launched BMX fit, a five-pocket model with a full, straight leg, is particularly appealing.

EVISU
Where? 9 Savile Row, London, W1 • 00 44 207 292 0500 • www.evisu.com
How much? From £142/$250/€207
This top-quality Japanese brand, born in a tiny tailor shop in Osaka, Japan, now delivers some of the best-quality denims in the world, all of which are housed in a recently opened store on London's Savile Row, where you can have jeans made-to-measure. The iconic Japanese label is designed by Burberry alumnus, Johnny Diamandis, and now features a new rainbow-coloured logo to prevent counterfeits.

IT'S ALL IN THE DETAIL
You can tell a lot about the quality of a pair of jeans by looking at the details. The **selvage** is the white stripe running down the seam, which seals the edge of the denim to prevent it fraying – experts can tell the brand and quality of the denim just by looking at this; New Yorkers actually show them off by rolling their jeans up. **Rivets** are the little metal studs used to reinforce the pockets and prevent wear and fraying. The **rise** is the distance between the crotch and the waistband. In many ways, the **back pocket** is now more important than the cut – it's the telltale sign of the brand and the position is instrumental in flattering the bottom. **Washes** are getting ever more complex, the older and more worn your jeans look, whether through sandblasting, rock washing or punching with holes, the more expensive they are likely to be.

CULT CLASSIC: LEVI'S 501S

Who hasn't owned a pair of trusty old Levi's 501s at some point? They are, without doubt, the most classic and iconic jeans ever and while not exactly the height of fashion, the Levi's 501 will probably be around for much longer than many of the flashy young jeans currently on the market. Levi Strauss was a Jewish Bavarian immigrant who hooked up with a tailor Jacob Davis in San Francisco to create men's trousers that wouldn't rip. Jacob had the brainwave of introducing rivets at points of strain, like on the pocket corners and base of the button fly. Although denim originates from 17th century France, and American men had worn denim

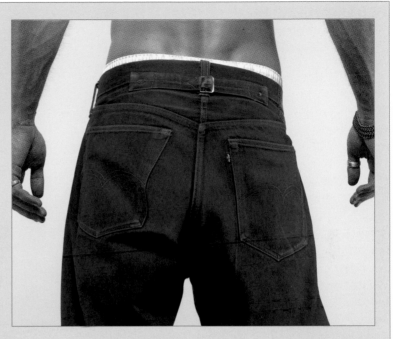

trousers without rivets for much of the 19th century, 1873 – the year Levi Strauss & Co. patented denim jeans with rivets – is viewed as the official birth date of blue jeans. The number 501 was assigned to the jeans in 1890 and the red tab was later added in 1936 to help identify them from a distance. The double row stitching on the back pockets, known as the Arcuate stitching design, is the oldest apparel trademark still in use today; it was first used in 1873 and during the Second World War, when it was painted on the pockets due to government rationing of essential items such as thread. Since 1966, reinforced stitching has replaced the back pocket rivets. A Levi's red tab with a capital E indicates they are pre-1971. Levi's bought a pair of 1890 501s for $25,000 (£14,340) in 1997. Today, a typical pair of 501s takes 3 metres (3¼ yards) of denim, five buttons, six rivets and 37 separate sewing operations.

Still stuck for choice?

Bodymetrics Have your body scanned using 'virtual fashion' technology to determine the perfect-fitting jeans. Selfridges, 400 Oxford Street, London, W1, and branches • 00 44 8708 377 377

Barneys 'Jeans Genies' will help you find the jeans of your dreams. www.barneys.com

Cantaloup Destination Denim on New York's Upper East Side carries innovative labels like Tsubi, Sacred Blue and Oligo Tissew. 1359 Second Avenue, New York, NY 10021 • 00 1 212 288 3569

Fred Segal is a jeans haven in LA, the epicentre for jeans production. 8100 Melrose Avenue, Los Angeles, CA 90046 • 00 1 323 655 3734

Henri Bendel's 'Denim Dream Team' will get you kitted out with divine denim. 712 Fifth Avenue at 56th Street, New York, NY 10019 • 00 1 212 247 1100

Brix Smith-Start at Shoreditch boutique Start can usually find you the jeans of your dreams just by looking at you. 59 Rivington Street, London, EC2 • 00 44 207 739 3636

Knickers / Panties

Agent Provocateur

Where?
6 Broadwick Street, London, W1 • 00 44 207 429 0229 • www.agentprovocateur.com
How much?
From £25/$45/€37

For women, a pair of knickers is one of the most personal, secretive and simultaneously exciting of purchases. Agent Provocateur, who made spending upwards of £20 on a pair of knickers acceptable, still offers one of the most pleasurable knicker-buying experiences thanks to their well-trained staff and exquisitely sexy selection. Established by Vivienne Westwood's son Joe Corre and his girlfriend Serena Rees in 1994, with the aim of creating the perfect lingerie store, Agent Provocateur's first shop in Soho's Broadwick Street is glamorous and stylish. The finely made silk and lace knickers are still some of the best you can find.

Agent Provocateur

SABBIA ROSA
Where? 71–73 Rue des Saints-Pères, 75006, Paris, France • 00 33 1 45 48 88 37
How much? From £35/$62/€50
This elegant French lingerie shop has served the likes of Madonna, Kate Moss and Catherine Deneuve, who no doubt adore the fine silk smalls and exquisite handmade lingerie. Naomi Campbell often buys up the whole collection. This label is luxurious to the max and super indulgent.

LA PERLA
Where? 163 Sloane Street, London, SW1 • 00 44 207 245 0527 • www.laperla.com
How much? From about £30/$55/€45
This Italian brand makes knickers in top-quality lace and pleated tulle, with a cinematic glamour and screen-star appeal in sexy black or more neutral beiges and creams.

The world's most comfortable pants

If it's simply a fabulously flattering pair of knickers you're after, the kind that won't expose any lumps and bumps or peep above the waistband of jeans and skirts, we have three recommendations. **Cosabella** (www.cosabella.com) is an Italian brand that produces the archetypal knicker shape in sheer colours, while **Elle Macpherson Intimates** (www.ellemacphersonintimates.co.nz) do a fantastic low-slung range that flatters the figure to no end. British company **Bodas** (www.bodas.co.uk) also offers an excellent range of neutrally toned knickers with minimal seams to prevent the dreaded VPL.

Little black dress

Roland Mouret

Where?
www.rolandmouretshowroom.co.uk • Department stores
worldwide, including Liberty and Selfridges
How much?
From £975/$1,727/€1,426

Slipping into one of Roland Mouret's finely sculpted dresses is like seeing yourself in a new, grown-up, film star context, one that's more than likely to have your lover drooling. Mouret's frocks change your posture, forcing you to put your shoulders back, breasts out and defining your waistline to perfection. 'Like a spell' is how some women have described them and Nicole Kidman, Gwyneth Paltrow, Dita von Teese and Scarlett Johansson are just some of the names to have fallen for Mouret's designs.

The son of a French butcher, Mouret was born in Lourdes in 1961. He presented his first collection of just 15 pieces to huge acclaim in 1998, describing his designs as 'the way a woman wraps herself in a sheet having just made love'. Mouret, who ceases designing under his own label after 2007, has evolved his method of draping and folding to create the ultimate little black dress, and right now you simply can't get better. Snap these modern-day classics up while you can.

LANVIN
Where? 22 Rue du Fauborg St-Honoré, 75008, Paris, France • 00 33 1 44 71 31 73 •
108 New Bond Street, London, W1 • 00 44 207 499 2929 • www.lanvin.com
How much? From £800/$1,459/€1,187
In 1920, Jean Lanvin launched her fashion label in Paris. She excelled at designing romantic fantastical dresses at a time when contemporaries like Chanel and Vionnet were intent on creating simple, modern clothes. Designer Albert Elbaz, who cut his teeth at Yves Saint Laurent in the mid-1990s, has revived her romantic spirit, injecting modernity into his ultra-desirable cinch-waist dresses that appear seamless and fit the female form beautifully.

ROCHAS
Where? 33 Rue François ler, 75008, Paris, France • 00 33 1 53 57 22 00 •
www.rochas.com
How much? From £800/$1,459/€1,187
In 1946, Marcel Rochas made his mark on fashion when he launched the guepiere – a long-line strapless brassiere that enclosed the hips. The label's current designer, Olivier Theyskens, has updated the look with sinewy, slim-fitting evening dresses that are as glamorous as they get.

Roland Mouret's modern-day classic 'Galaxy' dress

'A dress can be the expression of a state of mind. There are dresses that sing of joy of life, dresses that weep, dresses that threaten. There are gay dresses, mysterious dresses, pleasing dresses and tearful dresses.'

Paul Poiret, designer, 1879–1944

Lanvin's chic, belted LBD

Rochas' figure-hugging LBD

THE ORIGINS OF THE LITTLE BLACK DRESS

In 1919, Coco Chanel put black in fashion. Seven years later, *American Vogue* illustrated the Chanel 'Ford', calling it the 'frock that all the world would wear'. It was a sleeveless, black crepe-de-chine dress with a pin-tucked front, and thus the little black dress was born. Many have evolved the look. In the 1950s, French couturier, Jacques Fath, created elegant dresses to flatter the hourglass figure; in the 1960s, the LBD became truly fashionable once more with the space-age mini-dress look, epitomized by Twiggy and designer Paco Rabanne. In the late 1960s and 1970s, British designer Jean Muir made the 'little nothing' of a black dress a classic. As she said: 'When you have found something that suits you and never lets you down, why not stick to it?'

In the 1980s, Azzedine Alaia created the figure-hugging black Lycra dress. Nowadays, it's up to designers such as Roland Mouret, Albert Elbaz and Olivier Theyskens to push the LBD into the 21st century, with style, polish and aplomb.

www.thatperfectlittleblackdress.com
A brilliant website that sells a well-edited selection of elegant vintage black dresses from the 1940s to 1990s.

Pyjamas

Derek Rose

Where?
15 Savile Row, London, W1 •
00 44 207 434 3482 •
www.derek-rose.com

How much?
From £99.99/$180/€146

Derek Rose

We're currently in the grip of a pyjama boom. Thanks to the recent trend for 'relaxation' gear and men rediscovering the joys of nightwear, sales rose by over 20 per cent in 2004. Derek Rose is the undisputed king of pjs. His collection is worn by everyone from the Queen to the children at Hogwarts in the 'Harry Potter' films – even John and Yoko had matching his-and-hers pairs.

The Savile Row company, which was founded in 1926, specializes in tailored pyjamas – a flattering and generous cut, an elasticated waist, and a draught-proof array of buttons – in essence everything you could want from the perfect pyjama. The blue satin stripe with a single pocket and white piping is their bestseller, and since the company started a woman's line, the pink satin stripe is doing a roaring trade, too. The key is Rose's insistence that the satin is made from two-fold yarn, which gives the cloth more depth as well as ensuring it lasts longer. Also popular are the company's silk designs – *very* Cary Grant – as well as the military-influenced Regimental Stripe collection: with names like Black Watch and Brigade of Guards. After all, at some point everyone ends up a weekend guest – and 4am visits to the bathroom in a faded Snoopy T-shirt just won't do.

LAURENCE TAVERNIER

Where? 32 Rue du Bac, 75007, Paris, France • 00 33 1 49 27 01 69 • 77b Walton Street, London, SW1 • 00 44 207 823 8737 • www.laurencetavernier.com
How much? From £107/$188/€159
This French luxury label is dedicated to nightwear, making soft, cotton pyjamas, which are surprisingly elegant, yet still comfortable; as well as woollen bed coats, cashmere robes, slippers and bed socks. A range that is chic enough to wear outside the house – just about.

BROOKS BROTHERS

Where? Liberty Plaza, One Liberty Plaza, New York, NY 10006 • 00 1 212 267 2400 • Lion Plaza, 1 Old Bond Street, London, EC2 • 00 44 207 256 0013 • www.brooksbrothers.com
How much? £38/$70/€57
Brooks Brothers' candy-stripe pyjamas are the ones Madonna wore when photographed at home in bed with her children – in matching pairs – for *US Vogue*. Perfectly preppy, they're made from soft cotton with a darker blue piping and a drawstring waist.

Raincoat

Burberry trenchcoat

Where?
21–23 New Bond Street, London, W1 • 00 44 207 839 5222 • www.burberry.com
How much?
From £695/$1,280/€1,022

It's hard to pinpoint exactly what makes the Burberry trenchcoat such a timeless classic – the hint of checked lining perhaps? The simple belted form? The smart military epaulettes? In the early 1900s, army officers started wearing these coats as part of their uniform, and, by the 1940s, the trenchcoat had filtered into mainstream fashion. Today, the Burberry trench is still made from a closely woven Egyptian cotton called gabardine. It remains the best-loved raincoat there is, with all its authentic details still intact, such as the metal D-rings on the belt. Burberry's current Creative Director, Christopher Bailey, updates the style each season, reviving it with long or short hemlines, in a variety of colours and fabrics, including luxurious leather, suede and tweed. And, for the ultimate raincoat, you can now get your very own bespoke Burberry trench, made up to your specific shape and size. You can even get your intials embroidered onto the lining.

Burberry trenchcoat

MACINTOSH
Where? 54–55 Burlington Arcade, London, W1
How much? From £495/$885/€725
Created in the late 19th century, Macintosh is the original waterproof coat, made from a waterproof woollen fabric that was patented in 1829 by Charles Macintosh and Charles Goodyear. The classic British company now offers a made-to-measure service at the flagship London store.

AQUASCUTUM
Where? 100 Regent Street, London, W1 • 00 44 207 675 8200 • www.aquascutum.co.uk
How much? £650/$1,163/€725
In 1851, John Emary opened a small, high-quality tailors shop on Regent Street and in 1883 created the first rain-repellent cloth, naming it Aquascutum, taken from the Latin for water and shield, which subsequently became the name of his clothing brand. Emary went on to make a coat for King Edward VII in the late 1890s and then created trenchcoats for soldiers – and Winston Churchill. The contemporary Aquascutum range includes modern takes on the classic trench, but if it's a traditional style you're after, go for the classic Kingsgate design, available in navy, dark beige and black.

Shirt

Charvet

Where?
28 Place Vendôme, 75001, Paris, France • 00 33 1 42 60 30 70

How much?
Bespoke shirts from approximately £110/$200/€163

Housed in an elegant seven-floor building in Paris' Place Vendôme, Charvet is undisputedly the centre of the universe for shirt aficionados. Apart from the fact that it is reputed to have the largest selection of shirt fabrics in the world – they have 400 different shades of white and at least 200 different blues to choose from – the cut is impeccable. With its squared-off bottom, smart collar, elegant cuffs and solid buttons, a Charvet shirt looks as good with a bespoke suit as it does under a lambswool v-neck sweater.

Charvet's fine cotton shirts

TURNBULL & ASSER

Where? 71 & 72 Jermyn Street, London, SW1 • 00 44 207 808 3000 • www.turnbullandasser.com

How much? From £140/$255/€208: minimum of six shirts for first order.

Worn by prime ministers and princes alike (it's rumoured that the Sultan of Oman ordered 240 shirts in 20 minutes), this renowned British label was established in 1885 and offers the highest-quality shirts you can find in the UK. Choose from 1,000 different cloths, ranging from plain white poplin to voile, and brushed cotton to silk. What sets these shirts apart from the competition is the classic deep-spread collar, three-button barrel cuff, white lining and deep buffalo-horn buttons.

SIMONE ABBARCHI

Where? Borgo Santissimi Apostoli 16, Borgo Santissimi, Florence, Italy • 00 39 055 210 552
How much? From £55/$101/€122

The Italian tailor makes 3,000 shirts a year and has a loyal client base from London to LA. Customers start with a 25-minute consultation, during which measurements are taken and sample swatches shown. All the shirts are made exclusively from Italian cotton, linen, and silk.

Silk

Jim Thompson Thai Silk Company

Where?

9 Surawong Road, Bangkok, Thailand • 00 66 26 32 8100 • www.jimthompson.com

How much?

From £85/$150/€124 per metre

There's a wealth of choice at the Xiushui Silk Market in Beijing or at Varanasi in India, where many of the silks are interwoven with golden thread, but if you're serious about silk shopping, nowhere beats Thailand. Thai silk may be rougher in texture and heavier than silk made in China or India, but its quality is second to none, thanks to the country having the best soil in which to cultivate mulberry bushes (the leaves of which make up a silk worm's diet) and because the producers maximize the length of time a cocoon is boiled.

American Jim Thompson's name and shop are part of Thai legend, the rolls of silk displayed according to shade and hue and sold by the yard. For anyone after the finished product, there are also cushions, bedspreads, silk box-lamps that glow like candles and a selection of ready-to-wear dresses, shirts and ties. For something more bespoke, buy silk here and then take it to one of the hundreds of tailors dotted around the city.

Jim Thompson's has recently undergone a facelift, its slick new interior the work of hot, London-based designer Ou Baholyodhin. Ou is also behind a range of butter-soft leather goods in sugared-almond shades, as well as silk cushions, quilts and wooden furniture. Ou's items are often used in shoots for international design magazines – a small selection of his products are available at the Chelsea Harbour Design Centre in London and Maison et Objet in Paris – proof that this is a design company on the up and up.

And if that wasn't enough, the top floor is devoted to Thai antiques, everything from intricately carved miniature boxes to chests of drawers fit for a palace bedroom. Jim Thompson has also branched out into stylish bars, opening a number around Bangkok, thus further spreading the word in tasteful Thai living. For the ardent bargain hunter, there's a Jim Thompson factory outlet at Sukhumvit Soi 93.

Jim Thompson's Kaleidoscope

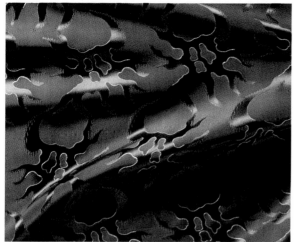
Jim Thompson's Sathorn

Jim Thompson's Venus new silk twill

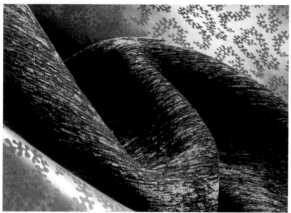
Jim Thompson's Paradise

OCKPOPTOK

Where? www.ockpoptok.com

How much? From £5/$8.90/€7.40

Meaning 'East meets West', this label was set up in 2000 by Jo Smith, a fashion photographer from London, and local girl, Veo Duangdala. Based in Luang Prabang, the weaving capital of Laos – where the silk is said to be of particularly high quality, all the better to take strong colours – the company uses only the finest silks and best quality natural dyes. OckPopTok has local weavers make up their products, which include clothes, wall hangings and cushions. No wonder their client list boasts both Kylie Minogue and Mick Jagger.

SABBIA ROSA

Where? 71–73 Rue des Saints-Pères, 75006, Paris, France • 00 33 1 45 48 88 37

How much? From £539/$946/€800 for a negligee

Rue des Saints-Pères is dotted with shops selling flimsy, fantasy underwear. The best is Sabbia Rosa – the place for the ultimate silk nightdress in a cornucopia of colours and prints, perfect for honeymooners. Devotees of the label include Gwyneth Paltrow, Elle MacPherson, and Madonna.

Tie

Hermès

Where?
Hermès stores worldwide • www.hermes.com

How much?
From £70/$128/€104

The tie: a curious invention and not entirely necessary. Well, it doesn't exactly serve much practical purpose now does it? The thing is, a shirt can look somewhat dull and vacant without one. A shirt and tie form an important sartorial partnership, and matching a shirt colour and pattern to the tie is essential. So too is the way a collar sits on the neck (it should be neither too low nor too high), the way the knot fills the spread (so that it isn't too fat or too skinny) and the way in which the blade covers the placket of the shirt front to finish on the waistband. Then there's the texture: a tie should be good to the touch – neither too floppy nor too rigid, but in a weighty, quality silk.

Hermès' classic ties

The classic Hermès tie is, for men, what their silk scarves are for women: refined, traditional and superior in quality. That discreet green and orange 'Hermès' label on the back is loaded with meaning – suggesting expense, refinement and wealth. The designs are classic with a twist and guaranteed to carry weight in the boardroom.

DUCHAMP
Where? 75 Ledbury Road, Notting Hill, London, W11 • 00 44 207 243 3970 • www.duchamp.co.uk
How much? £65/$118/€97
A relative newcomer to the tie scene, this dynamic British brand has injected a little life and soul into the market with vibrant, colourful designs made in silks of the highest quality. Duchamp has attracted quite a cult following as a result.

EMILIO PUCCI
Where? Department stores worldwide including Liberty and Neiman Marcus • www.pucci.com
How much? From £80/$178/€118
Vibrant Italian brand, Emilio Pucci, still designs some of the most iconic of ties in its signature swirly prints. Bold, bright and a flamboyant style statement in their own right. Search on eBay for classic and collectible 1960s' styles.

Duchamp's patterned ties

T-shirt

The plain and simple white T-shirt is probably the most widely worn garment in the world. So you would have thought it would be a cinch to find a good one, one that works in a variety of contexts and fits in all the right places – but it's not.

For women this means covering the midriff and skimming the top of your jeans with a fit that shows you have breasts without turning you into a contestant from a wet T-shirt competition. Sleeves are vital too – you don't want them to be too square and long, or you'll look like a throwback from a dodgy 1980s' pop band, and you don't want a capped sleeve, as that's not a T-shirt at all.

For guys, a T-shirt should neither be too baggy nor too tight. Ideally, you want it to hint at those sculpted pecks and leave the rest to the imagination.

T-shirts in every colour at American Apparel

T-shirt for men

Zimmerli of Switzerland

Where?

www.zimmerlitextil.ch

How much?

From £50/$88/€71

Established in 1871 by a needlework teacher named Pauline Zimmerli-Bauerlin, this Swiss luxury underwear brand – currently worn by Prince Charles, Tom Cruise and Karl Lagerfeld – has been at the forefront of developing the most luxurious T-shirts a man can buy. It's all down to their handling of fibres – using machines designed and made exclusively for the brand with delicate rod-twisted yarns that have been mercerized twice (a process in which the cotton thread is covered in polyester and treated in sodium hydroxide for added lustre and strength). The ultimate white T-shirt is from its 'Richelieu' collection – a shirt in 100 per cent mercerized cotton. Beautifully cut, soft but strong on the skin, it is sumptuous and practical too.

Mercerized cotton T-shirt, Zimmerli of Switzerland

AMERICAN APPAREL

Where? Stores worldwide including the US, UK, France, Canada, Mexico and Japan •
www.americanapparelstore.net
How much? From £10/$18/€15

This cool US T-shirt label's 2001 version of the fine, jersey short-sleeved classic T-shirt is slightly fitted and of a soft texture. Best of all, the label is firmly anti-sweatshops. The ethical consumer's choice.

HANES

Where? Department stores worldwide • 00 1 800 254 1545 • www.hanes.com
How much? From £5/$8/€6.50

As worn by Marlon Brando, this classic American T-shirt brand's short-sleeved 'Beefy T' in white features 100 per cent ringspun cotton, high-stitch density fabric and double-needled seams.

T-shirt for women

C&C California

Where?
Selected department stores worldwide, including Barneys, Bergdorf Goodman, Saks, Harvey Nichols and Selfridges •
www.candccalifornia.com
How much?
From £42/$75/€61

This relatively new label was founded by Los Angeles-based design duo Cheyann Benedict and Claire Stansfield in 2003. Their mission statement was to create the best T-shirt ever. They've done just that. Each of the 20 styles is made from ultra-fine combed cotton, so it moves and stretches in all the right ways, while feeling ultra-soft on the skin. There are now over 50 colours to choose from, with more being added all the time.

C&C's most perfect white T-shirt is the 'Classic Tee', which features a flattering, wider-than-usual crewneck, and also provides the perfect coverage over low-slung jeans. Lightweight and luxurious against the skin, it can be worn alone or layered beneath another. A wardrobe staple.

C&C California's 'Classic Tee'

C&C California's vibrant T-shirt collection

PETIT BATEAU

Where? 140 stores worldwide in Europe, Japan, Brazil and the US • www.petit-bateau.com
How much? From £14/$30/€24
A classic French kidswear label, set up in 1893, Petit Bateau's short-sleeved, scalloped crewneck T-shirt is as plain and simple as can be, with a classic cut and quality, thickish cotton.

Petit Bateau's simple T-shirt

GAP

Where? Stores worldwide • www.gap.com
How much? From £10/$10/€8
Gap's 'Favourite T-shirt' originated when the brand began in 1969 and remains a bestseller due to its classic cut, ample-width crewneck, just-right sleeves and durable thick white cotton.

*'T*he white T-shirt is just brilliant – it's universal, timeless and easy to wear. Wear it with jeans for an effortlessly chic style. It's the ultimate classic item.'*

Bay Garnett, fashion stylist

Gap's 'Favourite T-shirt'

Wedding dress

Vera Wang

Where?
Vera Wang Bridal House, 991 Madison Avenue, New York, NY 10021 • 00 1 212 628 3400 • www.verawang.com

How much?
From £1,600/$2,900/€2,411

Vera Wang

Since the early 1990s, Vera Wang has been the bridal label with the maximum kudos. Her dresses have a signature look, with clean lines and minimal fuss, yet they possess head-turning glamour. Wang treats the wedding aisle with the same attitude other designers treat the red carpet, and she has fittingly been the designer-of-choice for many an A-list bride – think Uma Thurman, Jessica Simpson and Sharon Stone – single-handedly forcing other more traditional wedding dressmakers to go back to the drawing board.

Frustrated at being unable to find a suitable dress for her own wedding, Wang spotted a niche in the market. In 1990, she opened her first boutique in the glitzy uptown Carlyle Hotel. The collection was an instant hit, with brides-to-be swooning over the expensive fabrics and exquisite detailing like delicate hand-sewn beading. More than anything, though, they adore Wang's vision of the modern bride, a career woman, quite possibly older than brides of yore, looking for a suitably sophisticated and grown-up dress.

Vera Wang still has a showroom at the Carlyle, a space that's considered by many as the ultimate bridal salon. And since she has so many imitators, her gowns now come with a certificate of authenticity. Wang has also branched out into non-bridal clothes as well as perfume and eyewear, but it is wedding dresses for which she will be forever known. Her Manhattan sample sales remain the stuff of legend – bridezillas have been known to travel across continents to fight tooth and claw for a heavily discounted gown, many of them one-of-a-kind samples.

STEWART PARVIN
Where? 14 Motcomb Street, London, SW1 • 00 44 207 235 1125 • www.stewartparvin.com
How much? From £2,000/$3,500/€2,900 for a dress from the diffusion line • From £8,000/$14,00/€11,700 for a bespoke dress
As one of the Queen's favourite designers, Parvin's well-heeled clientele know they're getting quality. They are also getting timeless style; his designs are strong and structured with razor-sharp lines. There is both a bespoke and a diffusion line. Parvin's promise is a couture-looking gown, even if it's off the peg.

MONIQUE L'HUILLIER
Where? www.moniquelhuillier.com
How much? Approximately £4,000/$7,000/€5,900
Since starting her company in 1996, Monique L'Huillier's range of gowns – romantic, dreamy, with a subtle sexuality – has gone from strength to strength. Many have a long silk sash, adding a welcome splash of colour to the bridal outfit.

Food & drink

'Eating is not merely a material pleasure. Eating well gives a spectacular joy to life and contributes immensely to goodwill and happy companionship. It is of great importance to the morale.'

Elsa Schiaparelli, fashion designer, 1890–1973

Balsamic vinegar

Giuseppe Giusti Aceto Balsamico Tradizionale

Where?

Viale Trento Trieste, 25–41100 Modena, Italy • 00 39 05 92 10 712 • www.giusti1605.com •

Good delis and gourmet websites worldwide, including: www.deandeluca.com and www.clubsauce.com

How much?

From £11/$20/€16 for a basic vinegar to upwards of £100/$176/€145

Giuseppe Giusti

It might seem surprising today, but balsamic vinegar wasn't on sale commercially until the 1960s. Before then, this 'black gold' was a well-kept secret, the sole preserve of Italian housewives lucky enough to know a decent producer. Nowadays, it's available in supermarkets all over the world, although for the most part it isn't actually balsamic vinegar, instead, it's a mixture of wine vinegar, caramel and colourings, a concoction that tastes astringent when compared to the real thing. Grapes should be the only ingredient.

The good stuff should be as dark as treacle and almost as thick, the taste a balance of sweet and sour. The general rule is the older the vinegar, the better. There are two key terms to look out for: *'tradizionale'*, which means it has been aged for at least 12 years, and 'D.O.C.', meaning it comes from a controlled denomination. You also need to check the provenance, as proper balsamic vinegar can only come from Modena in Italy, where they have stringent rules, similar to the appellation system for wines in France. Wax stamps placed over the corks are colour-coded in relation to age: red and white for vinegars at least 12 years old, silver for at least 18 years old and gold for 25 years old or more. Particulary old and therefore high quality vinegars will have a distinctive short and stocky bottle and stand.

You really can't go wrong with any aged balsamic vinegar from Modena. One of the oldest is Giusti, a family business that has been going since the early 17th century. The whole range is recommended, in particular their 40-year-old vintage, the perfect gift for any gourmand. Giusti's vinegar has been described as 'sweet, warm and wooded with a tart finish'. Buy from the family's Modena store, once frequented by Verdi.

LEONARDI ACETO BALSAMICO DI MODENA

Where? Good international delis • www.manicaretti.com • www.limoncello.co.uk
How much? From approximately £18/$32/€26
Produced by Giovanni Leonardi, a family business established in 1871, and another good name to look for.

CAVALLI 'CONDIMENTI BALSAMIC'

Where? Acetaia Ferdinando Cavalli, 6/ab Via del Cristo, Fellegaro di Scandiano, Italy • 00 39 05 22 983 430 • www.vendaravioli.com • www.cooksshophere.com • Good international delis
How much? Approximately £9.70/$17/€14
Not strictly balsamic vinegar, but the best commercial balsamic 'dressing' you will find. Made in Scandiano, Cavalli uses old barrels for flavour, some dating back to the 18th century. Chefs use it for marinating and seasoning salads.

Caviar

Almas Caviar

Where?

Various sources including: The Caviar House, 161 Piccadilly, London, W1 • 00 44 207 409 0445 • www.caviarhouse.com

How much?

Approximately £350/$616/€500 for 100g (3½oz)

Caviar is currently in a state of contention since the US put a ban on beluga imports. The reason behind this is the massively depleted numbers of beluga sturgeon; the population has fallen by 90 per cent in recent years due to overfishing, poaching and pollution. Caviar is the roe – or eggs – from one of 27 species of sturgeon. It is up to just three species to produce most of the world's supply: beluga sturgeon (beluga caviar), Russian sturgeon (osetra caviar) and stellate sturgeon (sevruga caviar).

Almas caviar

The most prized caviar is also the most rare. Almas, which is pale – almost white – in colour, comes from very rare albino sturgeons. Almas tastes creamy, smooth and almost buttery, and has an 18-month waiting list at The Caviar House in Piccadilly, where it is sold in a gold tin. In Iran, in fact, this caviar used to be the preserve of the Shah – and anyone else found eating it would have their right hand chopped off.

The delicate nature of *any* form of caviar means it should never be touched with any metal other than gold. Instead, serve the eggs using a mother-of-pearl spoon, the traditional utensil, although a wooden or plastic one will do; 14–28g (½–1oz) per person should suffice. Caviar is best eaten on blinis with sour cream. Gourmands suggest separating the caviar and sour cream, and eating each alternately on separate blinis to provide a delightful contrast. Wash down with a glass of champagne or a shot of vodka.

> '*Almas caviar is my favourite as it makes a great starter. In fact, I used it for the dinner I prepared for President Putin and Tony Blair.*'
>
> **Gordon Ramsay, chef**

BELUGA

Where? Various sources, including: www.imperialcaviar.co.uk

How much? Approximately £160/$282/€232 for 100g (3½oz)

Beluga caviar is another fine choice, in other words, the beluga that *isn't* Almas. Again, the taste is creamy and smooth – although not as buttery as the Almas – and the colour is a dark grey.

TSAR NICOULAI, CALIFORNIAN ESTATE OSETRA

Where? www.tsarnicoulai.com

How much? From £30/$53/€44 for a 28g (1oz) jar

When sturgeon were discovered living in Californian rivers, the American caviar industry revved into action. This is an excellent way for Americans to get around the US beluga ban. Osetra have larger eggs than beluga and are brown in colour, with a distinctive nutty taste.

Prestige selection caviar from Caviar House

Champagne

Louis Roederer Brut Premier

Where?
www.bbr.com • www.oddbins.com • All good wine merchants

How much?
Approximately £27/$47/€40

Louis Roederer Brut Premier

It would seem that we're all adhering to the famous creed of Lily Bollinger, who hailed from the champagne house of the same name and once said: 'I drink champagne when I'm happy, and I drink it when I'm sad… otherwise I never touch it – unless I'm thirsty.' Champagne consumption is higher now than ever before, especially among women, who are 13 times more likely to crack open the bubbly than men, making it no longer the preserve of special occasions.

So which one should you drink? The vast majority of wine writers rate Louis Roederer as the number one non-vintage champagne – it constantly tops blind tastings and was many an expert's recommendation as the best way to bring in the new millennium. Connoisseurs rave about its tiny, perfectly formed bubbles and clean taste, which has a creamy, buttery finish. Then there's the smell – a mix of toasted brioche and honey (many good champagnes have a distinct biscuity taste), combined with the scent of berries thanks to the profusion of pinot noir grapes – the proportion is roughly two to one pinot noir to chardonnay. Louis Roederer is also aged in wood, which is something of a rarity – most non-vintage champagnes are aged in stainless steel or glass containers – and comes from the same producer as the much more bling Cristal. Indeed, Cristal would have been number one if it wasn't so darned expensive – and its image wasn't so trashy, a problem its producers are well aware of. Brut Premier, on the other hand, is classy and accessible.

The best way to get your kick from champagne? Serve it at 7°C/45°F (any warmer, and the contents will foam excessively) from a flute glass that will preserve the bubbles. Drink it with caviar, oysters or smoked salmon – asparagus also complements the taste extremely well. The very, very best way to enjoy it, though, is to drink it on its own.

Cristal

CRISTAL

Where? www.bbr.com • All good wine merchants

How much? Approximately £125/$225/€183

P. Diddy famously spent £120,000 ($216,000) on Cristal in a London club – not as hard as you'd imagine when you consider the price. A cult name for quality quaffing.

KRUG GRAND CUVÉE

Where? www.bbr.com • All good wine merchants
How much? From £90/$157/€130

Dating back to 1843, this champagne house offers no entry-level bottles. 'We start where others stop,' they claim. Krug also has a distinctive taste: slightly dusty with hints of dried fruit, toasted brioche, roses and violets, a unique bouquet that's said to be the result of storing champagne in oak barrels.

Krug Grand Cuvée

PARLEZ-VOUS CHAMPAGNE?

Deciphering the label on a champagne bottle can be a perplexing experience, especially when the words are in French, and when 'extra dry' is not as dry as 'Brut' (meaning 'dry'). Confusing. Below is a brief guide to some key terms.

- **Blanc de blanc**: Champagne made using only white grapes, usually chardonnay. This is a classic aperitif champagne.
- **Blanc de noir**: Champagne made using black grapes, usually pinot noir; it tastes particularly good with food.
- **Brut**: Dry.
- **Brut nature**: Bone dry.
- **Cuvée**: Blend.
- **Cru**: Literally 'growth'. This also refers to the villages in the Champagne region that provide wines of exceptional quality.
- **Extra dry**: Not as dry as brut; a slight sweetness.
- **Grand cru**: 'Great growth'. This phrase is attributed to a vineyard with the very highest rating and also identifies the Champagne villages that produce the very best wine – 17 have been bestowed this status.
- **Grand marque**: A group of the biggest and most famous champagne names.
- **Mise en cave** (followed by date): The date the wine was cellared.
- **Non-vintage** (NV): A champagne mostly from a single year, but with older wines blended in. This is the most common form of champagne.
- **Premier cru**: A vineyard with the second highest rating.
- **Prestige cuvée**: A champagne house's most expensive champagne; some are vintage, others non-vintage.
- **Récoltant-manipulant (RM)**: An independent grower-producer; so not one of the grandes marques.
- **Vintage**: Champagne of a single, notably good year – 1990 and 1996 are considered the two best.

Chocolate

L'Artisan du Chocolat

Where?

89 Lower Sloane Street, London, SW1 • 00 44 207 824 8365 •
www.artisanduchocolat.com

How much?

Banana and thyme chocolate £7.50/$14/€10.50 for 12

L'Artisan du Chocolat

Multi-Michelin-starred chef Gordon Ramsay describes L'Artisan du Chocolat as 'the Bentley of chocolate' and theirs is the only range he will serve in his restaurants. Ditto Heston Blumenthal, owner of The Fat Duck, 'The Best Restaurant in the World 2005', according to *Restaurant* magazine. All of which is praise indeed, especially for such a young company (it has only been running since 1999) – and a British one, at that. Traditionally, the world's best chocolatiers have been confined to Belgium, Switzerland and France. The ambitious aim of the co-founder, Gerard Coleman, is to make L'Artisan du Chocolat the best in the world, while ensuring that quality is never, ever compromised; hence the company has no immediate plans for expansion. Indeed, the self-confessed perfectionist is behind the manufacture of every single chocolate and the company, like the ever-innovative Blumenthal, is known for its use of unusual ingredients – flavours include sesame, Bramley apple, green cardamom and tobacco. Banana and thyme is its bestseller, a thin shell of intense chocolate encasing two very different flavours that somehow balance each other magnificently. Coleman believes that part of his success is down to the British public's enthusiasm to try new things. 'They are more open to experimentation than the French, Belgians or Germans, who have more defined tastes and don't want you to start putting cardamom in their chocolate', he has said. Coleman, himself a chef by training, decided that Britain was missing a top-notch chocolatier. He spent time working with esteemed Belgian chocolate company Pierre Marcolini before branching out on his own. Each of his chocolates is freshly made and, once bought, should be stored at 15°C/59°F and eaten within a

L'Artisan du Chocolat

fortnight. Unlike most chocolatiers, who only use one bean, Coleman uses different beans to complement the different flavours of the centres, all of which are made using the finest raw ingredients. As well as taste, Coleman is also obsessed with texture – be it the crunch of a nutty praline or the silky smoothness of a berry filling – believing this to be another crucial factor in the making of perfect chocolate.

PIERRE MARCOLINI

Where? www.marcolini.be
How much? Orange thyme praline £5/$9/€7 for three
This Belgian chocolatier has been in business since 1990 and is one of the few who still processes all of his own cocoa beans – according to Belgian law, only producers who make their wares from scratch can technically call themselves 'chocolatiers'. He now has shops in London and Tokyo. Bestsellers include his praline, the orange-thyme combination a particular favourite.

LA MAISON DU CHOCOLAT

Where? www.lamaisonduchocolat.com
How much? Bacchus truffles from 70p/$1/€1 each
Robert Linxe of the Paris-based La Maison du Chocolat is known in the industry as 'the creator' and the original superstar chocolatier. He is obsessed with ganache, a gooey centre that is made from cream and chocolate, sometimes adding an infusion. The Bacchus truffle with rum and raisin filling is his self-confessed favourite; each raisin is 'tailed and flamed' before being impregnated with a rum vapour.

La Maison du Chocolat

Claret

Château Mouton Rothschild, 1945

Where?

Nickolls & Perks • www.nickollsandperks.co.uk

Wine Bid • www.winebid.com

Aficionado Cellars • www.aficionadocellars.com

Fine & Rare Wine • www.frw.co.uk

Berry Bros. & Rudd • www.bbr.com

How much?

Anything upwards of £3,000/$4,500/ 3,950 • Other vintages start at around £80/$141/€118

Château Mouton Rothschild

Did you know that the actual cost of the wine in a £4 ($7) bottle is usually only about 60p ($1)? Proof, if proof were needed, that when it comes to wine, it really does pay to pay more. But how much more? With claret – and vintage claret, at that – the costs can easily go into the thousands. First, a couple of clarifications: claret is a dry red wine from the Bordeaux region, dark in colour with a fruity, liquorice-tinged flavour. It is best when it matures – drinking it young won't always do it justice. A vintage claret refers to a year when the grapes achieved perfect ripeness. Despite claims to the contrary, there have only been three great claret vintages since the Second World War – 1945, 1961 and 1982. Of course, one never knows a truly great vintage until several years down the line, so when it comes to buying claret it is always worth taking risks.

Nowadays, more people than ever are interested in expensive wine, thanks in part to the influential wine critic Robert Parker and his '100-point' system, but also because of the burgeoning economies of China and Russia. Blue-chip chateaux still attract the most interest: think Château Lafite Rothschild, Château Latour or Château d'Yquem, which is famous for holding back some supplies for later sales. All are names worth noting when purchasing claret.

But what's the best? The answer, of course, is totally subjective – one man's Château Latour is another man's Ribena – but the respected wine magazine *Decanter* recently came up with a suggestion: Château Mouton Rothschild, 1945, the one wine their critics claimed everyone should 'drink before they die'.

The magazine described it as 'intense, concentrated, indescribable... without doubt the greatest claret of the 20th century'. Not bad for a château that only officially received 'Première Cru Classe' (the highest classi-fication possible) in 1973. The château lies opposite Lafite and has been growing vines since the 1720s. Mouton Rothschild's *terroir*, or soil, is formed of deep gravel beds with a subsoil consisting of clay and limestone. Their claret is made up of 85 per cent cabernet sauvignon, 10 per cent cabernet franc and five per cent merlot. Oenophiles can tour the château, taking in the original artwork by Picasso, but the cellar, which houses 35,000 bottles of untouched wine, some dating back to 1859, is strictly off-limits.

Incidentally, a tip for cheaper claret – and indeed red wine in general – is to decant it into a glass vessel before drinking. This will add oxygen, instantly making the most bog-standard bottle taste like a million dollars. A similar trick can be done with white using a ceramic jug to keep it cooler.

Château Cheval Blanc

CHÂTEAU PETRUS

Where? Corney & Barrow • www.corneyandbarrow.com
How much? From approximately £40/$70/€59

A Merlot-dominated claret that has risen to prominence, in part because Robert Parker is such a fan.

CHÂTEAU CHEVAL BLANC

Where? Berry Bros. & Rudd • www.bbr.com
How much? From approximately £47/$83/€69

A claret that's found fame for a very different reason – it featured in the acclaimed movie *Sideways*. According to Miles, the film's anti-hero, this is 'the only wine worthy of seducing a woman'. It has an unusually high percentage of cabernet franc grapes, which doesn't usually produce good wines on its own, except in the case of Château Cheval Blanc. The result is a lush, velvety texture with a slight truffle and mushroom tinge on the tongue. Unlike most clarets, you can drink this one relatively young – after seven or eight years – but ideally wait until it's around 20 years old. Ignore Miles when it comes to vintage, though; despite his claims to 1961, the ultimate is actually 1947. Parker gave this one 100 out of 100.

SIMON BERRY, OF THE QUEEN'S WINE MERCHANTS, BERRY BROS. & RUDD, CHATS ABOUT CLARET.

What makes claret so great?
Simon Berry: 'It's unique. Cabernet sauvignon is grown throughout the world, but the finest clarets are still the greatest wines in that they are never bettered. You might have to pay anything over £50 ($90) a bottle to get something fantastic – but with tickets to football matches costing that nowadays, it's not a lot for one of life's great luxuries.'

How should the perfect glass of claret taste?
SB: 'Almost indescribable – but with an extraordinary balance of fruit, acidity and density. It will have great complexity – a taste that changes and develops over time – and will linger in the mouth for a significant period. It's instantly recognizable, though, once you've experienced a few.'

What are good, more affordable options?
SB: 'The 1990s and 1989s are wonderful now. And great properties from 1997 are very affordable.'

For the first-time buyer, what advice would you give?
SB: 'Find a good wine merchant – someone who you trust, and who will take you through what will end up as a journey of discovery. And remember that it's all about personal taste. Really, the only important question is: is it good to drink?'

Coffee

Kopi Luwak.

Where?

Edible, 23-25 Redchurch Street, London, E2 • 00 44 207 739 1016
Selfridges, 400 Oxford Street, London, W1 and
branches • 00 44 8708 377 377 •
www.selfridges.co.uk • www.tastesoftheworld.net

How much?

Approximately £24/$42/€35 for a 57g (2oz)
bag.

A good cup of coffee should be treated in the same manner as a fine wine – sniffed, savoured and generally respected. Coffee was supposedly introduced into Europe in 1683 when the Turkish army left sackfuls of the stuff behind in haste as they retreated from the gates of Vienna. Since then, it has enjoyed unrivalled popularity. In 1996, for instance, an Italian court ruled that all government workers had the statutory right to a morning coffee break. And perhaps even more surprising is the fact that since 1988, the British have spent more on coffee than they have on tea. The best blend is down to personal taste, but the most expensive, the most rare and, therefore, the most covetable is that ground from the kopi luwak. These beans from Indonesia are produced in the most unusual way: from the excrement of tree-climbing civets who feast on coffee cherries, eating them whole, bean and all. When they have passed through their bodies, the bean remains, albeit covered in a parchment-like layer. The beans are then collected by locals, who remove the shell and sell them on.

The result, thanks to the civet's gastric juices, is a uniquely smooth flavour that many describe as reminiscent of caramel and chocolate without any hint of bitterness. Edible, the bean's main distributor in Britain, says customers include Damian Hirst.

Civet Coffee,
Kopi Luwak.

JAMAICAN BLUE MOUNTAIN

Where? The Tea and Coffee Plant, 180 Portobello Road, London, W11 • 00 44 207 221 8137 •
www.coffee.uk.com • www.tastesoftheworld.net • Reputable delis and food halls

How much? From £45/$79/€67 per kilo (2lb 3oz)

With the exception of the Kopi Luwak, Blue Mountain is the coffee synonymous with high prices. This is because the beans are so hard to reach – they grow 2,100 metres (6,890 feet) above sea-level in Jamaica's Blue Mountains. The result is a sweet, full-bodied cup. As always, single-estate is the best, but beware – there are lots of Blue Mountain imitators out there.

ORIGIN

Where? www.origincoffee.co.uk • 00 44 1326 340 320

How much? £3/$6/€5 per bag

Origin is not only a Fairtrade coffee, but it also tastes superb – the Cornish company's aim is to be the best in Britain, competing with the likes of Illy and Lavazza. It is already sold at some of the finest Cornish dining establishments – Rick Stein's Café and St Petroc's bistro in Padstow, for instance – and is spreading nationwide. Origin is also organic and has even obtained the seal of approval from the Rainforest Alliance, an organization that ensures good environmental and social practice. For those who prefer a conscience with their cuppa.

HOW TO ENJOY THE PERFECT CUP OF COFFEE:

Starbucks may produce a somewhat weak blend, but the company does employ a number of world-class coffee experts, all of whom are well-schooled in the intricacies of different beans. Here Andrew Reynolds, coffee education manager for Starbucks UK, gives a brief introduction to properly savouring and understanding coffee:

• 'To get the perfect cup of coffee at home there are a few steps to follow that can really make a difference. I recommend using a whole bean coffee and freshly grinding it before each brew. This will retain the freshness of flavour, since ground coffee will only be at its best for 24 hours.

• For a cafetière, the ground must be coarse. Use 10 level tablespoons (50g / 2oz) of coffee in a clean, eight-cup cafetière. Pour in hot, just-off-the-boil water and stir. Place the plunger loosely on the top and leave for four minutes exactly. Plunge slowly and serve immediately – the coffee will be at its best for the next 20 minutes.

• Enjoying the perfect cup of coffee may seem like one of the simple pleasures in life but the journey from the coffee bean to your cup is complex and artistic. For the best, most refined flavour only the finest Arabica beans, grown at altitudes above 900 metres (2,953 feet), will do. These are selected from farms throughout the tropics. Then begins the processing and roasting of the beans, an art form that determines the aroma, acidity and flavour of the coffee.

• Like wine, the aroma, flavour, acidity and body of the coffee can be explored through sophisticated cupping (tasting) methods. Your tongue can only distinguish four tastes; your nose, on the other hand, can detect thousands of aromas so make sure you smell your coffee first. That way you will be able to detect subtle influences, for instance nuts, lemons and spices.

• When tasting coffee, be sure to slurp as this sprays coffee over the tongue for an enhanced experience. Think about how the coffee tastes, its weight on your tongue and its acidity. Acidity can be high, medium and low and refers to the lively, palate-cleansing property that can be felt on the roof of the mouth or sides and top of the tongue rather than its PH value.

• Finally, coffee is grown all over the world, from South America to Indonesia, and again, like wine, the flavour is influenced by the climate, soil and conditions specific to each of these areas. This means that your perfect cup of coffee may be quite different to your friend's and there is no better way to discover your favourite than by trying coffees from different areas with different food pairings.

• Try a bold Kenyan coffee in the morning with berries and feel the sparkle in your mouth; serve an aged Sumatran coffee with a creamy cheese after dinner with a friend (my personal favourite); or pair Columbian coffee with a nutty granola bar for a mid-afternoon snack. But whatever you try, if you follow the basics, you can always enjoy the perfect cup of coffee.'

Ice cream

Corrado Costanzo

Where?
Via Spaventa 7, Noto, Sicily • 00 39 931 835 243

How much?
Prices from £1/$2/€1.40 a scoop

Gelato

Anyone with a sweet tooth should get the next flight to Sicily – an island where they even eat ice cream for breakfast, usually in the form of a hollowed-out brioche filled with *gelato*. Ice cream was invented here some time around the 8th century, when Arabs inhabiting the island first thought to scoop the ice from the slopes of Mount Etna, and combine it with sugar, milk and flavourings from local products, such as oranges, lemons, almonds and roses. The ideal way, they figured, to stave off the fierce summer heat.

The best gelato comes from the baroque town of Noto in the south of the island. Here you'll find the world's most mouthwatering scoops at Corrado Costanzo, a *gelateria* that has been running for almost 50 years. Along with the more traditional flavours like vanilla, chocolate and coffee, are more unusual concoctions made from mulberry, rose and jasmine. Like the Arabs, Costanzo is fastidious about preparing his puddings with the very best local ingredients, only using flowers picked in the evening, for instance, when they are at their most fragrant.

The bestseller, though, is *granita al mandarino*, a sorbet made with the juiciest local mandarin oranges, the result is the epitome of refreshing zinginess, and not in the least bit tart. People will travel for miles – continents, even – simply to sample what Costanzo calls 'the taste of Sicily in your mouth'. Of course this is not strictly an ice cream – but then neither is gelato, since gelato (italian ice cream), unlike most of that found in Britain and the US, is made using milk rather than cream.

HILL STATION

Where? www.hillstation.co.uk
How much? £4/$7/€6 for 500ml (17 fl oz)
This Wiltshire-based company is run by a well-travelled American couple and their ice cream is most punters' top deli choice. Their divine Fairtrade white chocolate flavour is exactly what it says on the tub, but Hill Station should really be praised for managing to make spicier flavours, such as cardamom, cinnamon and stem ginger, work so well.

ALBA GOLD

Where? 72 High Street, London, W3 • 00 44 208 992 5748 • Selected delis and restaurants worldwide
How much? £4/$7/€6 for 500ml (17 fl oz)
Alba Gold, a proper Italian artisan ice cream, is only available in small quantities since most is sold directly on to Michelin-starred restaurants. The company's ingredients are the finest available: pistachios from Sicily, for instance, or sun-matured strawberries from Morocco. The tiramisu flavour is exceptional.

Olive oil

Manni Per Me

*Manni
Per Me*

Where?

www.manni.biz • 00 39 69 72 74 787

How much?

£48/$85/€71 for 200 ml (7 fl oz)

There's everyday olive oil – the kind you use for cooking – and then there's the special stuff, the gourmet liquid gold reserved for drizzling, dipping and savouring. Manni Per Me is officially the world's most expensive oil olive, but, for once, the eyebrow-raising prices are in sync with quality, as this is also the world's very best.

The oil was created in 2000, when Italian filmmaker Armando Manni became a father for the first time and wanted to find the purest olive oil possible for his son. For this he needed science and enlisted the help of the University of Florence. Scientists there pinpointed the exact time the olives should be picked, when they would be at their richest in antioxidants and they would also have the fullest flavour. Manni bought some groves on Mount Amiata in southern Tuscany and put the research into practice.

The result of all this careful planning is two oils. *Per Mio Figlio* (for my child) is ideal for babies and young children – Madonna uses it for Rocco and Lourdes – and has a smooth, buttery taste. *Per Me* (for me) is for adults and has a full-flavoured and peppery taste. It's so rich, in fact, that enthusiasts claim you can use less oil than you normally would – which is one way to save money. Incidentally, the difference in taste between the two oils is because olives from higher up the mountain are used for *Per Me* as these have a more intense flavour. Production is limited to 2,500 litres (550 gallons) a year. The oil can only be purchased over the internet and is sent out in special temperature-controlled containers.

Giorgio Locatelli, of upscale pasta haven Locanda Locatelli in London, apparently went nuts upon his first tasting of Per Me, instantly ordering a huge batch for use in his restaurant. It is also used in Les Ambassadeurs at the Hôtel de Crillon in Paris, The Fat Duck in Bray and the Park Hyatt in Tokyo.

Chefs shout Manni's praise from the roofs of their Michelin-starred restaurants. 'It's a rare breed of person who strives for perfection in his chosen line of work', says Thomas Keller of the French Laundry in Napa Valley. 'Armando Manni personifies this determination – he has successfully produced the best and healthiest extra virgin olive oil on the market.'

'When I first tasted Manni's oils, I knew I had tasted something amazing.'

Jean-Georges Vongerichten of Vong and the Mercer Kitchen in New York

CASA PONS MAS PORTELL

Where? www.casaponsusa.net • www.tienda.com • www.earthy.com
How much? Approximately £3.50/$7/€5 for 250 ml (8.5 fl oz)
Spain is the biggest producer of olive oil in the world – it has around 370 million olive trees – and certain oil snobs prefer fruitier Spanish oils to Italian varieties. Pons, which has an almost almondy taste, is one of the best. All the olives are hand-picked, and the oil is made in a traditional stone mill in Catalonia. Each bottle is individually numbered.

NICOLAS ALZIARI

Where? 14 Rue St-François-de-Paule, 06300, Nice, France • www.alziari.com.fr • 00 33 4 93 85 76 92
How much? Approximately £8/$15/€11.50 for 500 ml (17 fl oz)
Few visitors leave Nice without buying this oil in its distinctive blue and yellow tin. Alziari uses small black olives crushed on a millstone that was powered by the neighbouring river until relatively recently. The resulting taste is gorgeously buttery. Use this to make the perfect salade niçoise.

Nicolas Alziari

A BRIEF GLOSSARY OF OLIVE OIL TERMS

Understanding the wording on a bottle of olive oil is a little like deciphering a bottle of wine – although it should be noted that, unlike wine, olive oil does not improve with age; instead it has a shelf life of about a year. The best are sold in coloured glass bottles, as light and heat can be harmful to the oil. Greener olive oils are made using olives earlier in the season – because they're not as juicy as when they are ripe, this type uses up more olives and is therefore more expensive.

- **Single estate:** From a single family business or farm. Two of the best in Tuscany are Capezzana and Badia a Coltibuono.
- **Blended:** An oil made using olives from different estates, varieties, regions, sometimes even countries.
- **First cold press:** Oil from the first pressing of the olives, with no applied heat.
- **Extra virgin olive oil:** Production is by hand or machine and no chemicals are used. This will have no more than one per cent acidity resulting in a fantastic aroma and flavour.
- **Virgin olive oil:** As above, but with an acidity of up to two percent.
- **Olive oil:** Has up to 3.3 per cent acidity. This is a lower quality since it's a blend of virgin olive oil and refined (oil that has been chemically treated to neutralize strong tastes). The most common olive oil.
- **Unfiltered:** Contains small bits of olive; will have lots of flavour but sediment at the bottom.

Spice

MM Spices

Where?
M/S Mahesh Kumar Mohan Das, Shop
No 206/3, Clock Tower, Jodhpur, India
How much?
From £1/$2/€1.40

MM Spices

India is the motherland of spice – venture into any market and you can smell the spice-sellers selling sachets from hessian sacks a mile off. The only problem is the bewildering array before you, coupled with merchants understandably unused to dealing with curious foreigners.

Which is where MM Spices comes in. The Jodhpur shop, close to the main square, is both accessible and fun. It even has celebrity endorsement – the actor Jeremy Irons often visits Jodhpur for antiques, the other ware for which the city is famous, and will pop here for some seasoning. Plus the proprietor, King Rose, is one shopkeeper you won't forget in a hurry. This self-styled Bollywood hero, complete with medallion, moustache and a pair of jeans that leaves nothing to the imagination, is the ultimate salesman. The result? It's virtually impossible to leave empty-handed.

Luckily, this is one of the best spice shops in India and sells its stock to restaurants nationwide. King Rose sits customers down on a plastic stool and propels them into sensory overload, encouraging them to smell, taste and touch his entire stock, from powdered turmeric, saffron, cinnamon bark and a million varieties of tea, to the 'winter tonic', a sort of natural viagra for men.

Amateur cooks can pick up bags of masala, a blend of different spices, for about 250 rupees (£3/$6/€4), including an easy recipe for making the most out-of-this-world curry. All this *and* a drawstring silk bag to carry home your wares.

HERBORISTERIE AVENZOAR
Where? 78 Bis Derb N'Khel, Rahba Lakdima, Marrakech, Morocco
How much? From £1/$2/€1.40
The world's other great spice centre is Morocco. In Marrakech, ask your guide to direct you to Herboristerie Avenzoar for good-quality spices, as well as massages using different plant oils.

THE SPICE SHOP
Where? 1 Blenheim Crescent, London, W11 • 00 44 207 221 4448 • www.thespiceshop.co.uk
How much? From £1/$2/€1.40
This tiny Notting Hill shop has the best all-round selection of spices in Britain, including unusual choices such as jade seaweed salt and four types of cumin. The owner travels the world sourcing the very best spices, while gaining a specialist knowledge that's second to none. The shop also has an excellent mail order service.

Tea

Silver Needles

Silver Needles tea

Where?

Various specialist teashops and tea websites, including:
www.theteatable.com and www.greysteas.co.uk •
Claridge's tearoom, Brook Street, London, W1 •
00 44 207 629 8860

How much?
£4/$7/€6 per 28g (1oz)

Of all liquids consumed by the world's population, 40 per cent is tea. And whether black or green, it all comes from the same source – the leaves of the shrub *camellia sinensis*. Variations are down to the treatment: black tea is fermented, green is steamed and dried and oolong is partially fermented – the oxidation process is stopped before it is complete.

The British are probably best known for their love of tea, especially given their mindset – that a cup of tea and sympathy can solve just about any problem. Tea first came to Britain in 1644, thanks to the East India Company, and by the 18th century it had become the country's most popular beverage. So much so that following the Boston Tea Party, patriotic Americans showed their allegiance to their country by swapping tea-drinking for coffee.

For a really special brew, connoisseurs should try Silver Needles, one of the rarest teas – and therefore one of the most expensive. It is also a white tea, a type that has become increasingly popular in recent years due to the fact that it's packed full of antioxidants – up to three times more than green, in fact.

White tea is made from immature tea leaves that must be picked before the buds are fully opened. Silver Needles comes from the Fujian Province of China and is picked within a two-day period in early spring. The tea gets its name from the dried leaves, which are needle-shaped and silver in colour due to the fuzz that still covers the bud. The result is a tea admired for its full-bodied and exceptionally delicate flavour.

Once the preserve of the Chinese Emperor and *nobody* else – 900 years ago, during the Song Dynasty, a cup of this tea would have cost you your head – it is now readily available over the internet.

FORTNUM & MASON

Where? 181 Piccadilly, London, W1 • 00 44 207 734 8040
How much? From £7/$12/€10 for a 250g (8oz) tin
The upmarket grocer has a rare tea bar that sells one of the best selections of uncommon teas in the world. Popular varieties include rose pouchong, Russian caravan and Margaret's Hope.

MARIAGE FRÈRES

Where? 30 Rue du Bourg-Tibourg, 75004, Paris, France • 00 33 1 42 72 28 11 • www.mariagefreres.com
How much? £82/$144/€120 per 100g (3½oz)
Another excellent purveyor of tea is Mariage Frères, a Parisian company that sells over 50 types of Darjeeling. Brumes d'Himalaya ('Himalayan mists') is their most expensive; the leaf tips are picked from the 'first flush' (i.e. the first spring harvest) at a single estate in Darjeeling. Incidentally, most 'Darjeeling' sold in shops is nothing of the kind, since it comes from Kenya or Sri Lanka. Beware of imitations.

Vodka

Jean-Marc XO

Where?
www.jeanmarcxovodka.com • All good food-halls and off-licences

How much?
£28/$50/€42 for a standard bottle

Russian, Swedish, Polish – which vodka is the best? French, actually. Jean-Marc XO has none of the vodka 'afterburn' (the feeling as the liquid travels down the throat) that's so familiar with many Eastern European brands. This is because it is made in the same manner as cognac (hence the 'XO'). Indeed, the brand recently won a prestigious taste test when the US Beverage Tasting Institute rated it the best vodka ever, with a score of 96 out of 100.

The company was started by Jean-Marc Daucourt, a French distiller from Cognac. 'Vodka isn't big in France,' he explains, 'but I discovered it 20 years ago when I lived in America, and knew that we could do better.'

Using the same copper stills that are used in the cognac-making process, the vodka is distilled nine times to remove all the impurities – most vodkas are distilled twice at the most – then micro-oxygenated to further kill the afterburn. Jean-Marc Daucourt is the only company in the world that does this. The result is the perfect vodka – clear, with floral notes, anise and a pleasingly powdery feel in the mouth. Best of all, it doesn't taste too alcoholic – it's as odourless and as flavourless as it gets, the way vodka ought to be. In fact, you can merrily drink Jean-Marc XO on the rocks without wincing.

Jean-Marc XO

GREY GOOSE
Where? All good off-licences
How much? £30/$54/€45
The world's most popular super-premium brand is also blended and bottled in Cognac. The making of the company was winning a taste test in 1998 – the same one Jean-Marc XO pipped them to more recently. A favourite with many top mixologists, Grey Goose has a creamy taste and is widely available.

BELVEDERE
Where? All good off-licences
How much? £27/$49/€40
Another popular super-premium brand, Belvedere is made in Poland from rye (most Polish vodka comes from potatoes). The taste is creamy with hints of vanilla, and is the bling vodka choice – a long-standing favourite with the hip-hop community.

Health & beauty

'The best thing is to look natural, but it takes a lot of makeup to look natural.'

Calvin Klein, fashion designer, 1942–

Aftershave

Creed Green Irish Tweed

Where?

38 Avenue Pierre 1er de Serbie, 75008, Paris, France • 00 33 1 47 20 58 02 •
www.creedfragrances.co.uk

How much?

£66/$121/€97

Green Irish Tweed is Creed's bestselling fragrance for gentlemen – that is gentlemen with a capital G. The aftershave was originally created for none other than Cary Grant, surely the original chap. Wearers today are just as suave: George Clooney, Pierce Brosnan, Robbie Williams, David Beckham – even Prince Charles is a fan.

Part of Green Irish Tweed's charm is the way it smells so light – there's no overpowering afterburn here. The balanced blend of floral, green and woody notes include verbena, violet leaves, Florentine iris, sandalwood and ambergris. It could be said that Creed started the current trend for bespoke scents, as all but two of their fragrances were originally made exclusively for their wearers. Spring Flowers, for instance, was created for Audrey Hepburn, while Madonna has spent thousands and waited three years for Creed to make her own couture scent, a process that is based on the wearer's personality, passions and olfactory preferences. Creed, established in 1760, is one of only a handful of perfume houses still privately owned. The current owner, Oliver Creed, is something of a scent obsessive, sourcing the

*Creed Green
Irish Tweed*

purest essence of rose from Bulgaria and Morocco, jasmine and irises from Italy, tuberose from India and genuine Parma violets. The most expensive of these is the Bulgarian rose, which costs £28,000 to £44,000 per kilo ($50,000 to $80,000 for 2lbs), more than 30 times the price of beluga caviar.

Creed still makes all of its perfumes using the traditional infusion technique. The components are weighed, mixed and filtered by hand, then left to seep for weeks, while Oliver tinkers to make each batch perfect. The oils used are always slightly different, which means that the scents vary in fragrance year on year, rather like a fine wine. Experts claim you can instantly distinguish a Creed fragrance, as their scents are notably deeper, richer and more eccentric than any others. In fact, many Creed scents are initially rejected by department store buyers for smelling too unusual. To appreciate Creed, it would seem, takes time, as most of the rejected fragrances end up bestsellers. Creed also takes a deep pocket – developing a passion for their fragrances is an expensive habit, but, given the company of their wearers, it is well worth it.

Parfums de Nicolai New York

PARFUMS DE NICOLAI NEW YORK
Where? www.beautyhabit.com • www.thesenteurs.com
How much? £35/$65/€51
Made by Patricia de Nicolai, the granddaughter of Pierre Guerlain, the esteemed nose Dr Luca Turin describes this, one of his favourite aftershaves, as 'more a companion for life than a mere perfume, a hugely complex and exquisitely balanced citrus-warm composition that never shouts but glows mysteriously at close range'. Indeed the spicy scent, the ingredients of which include bergamot, cloves, amber and vetiver, is highly coveted by knowledgeable cologne-lovers. Quite an achievement given that Parfums de Nicolai receives scant publicity.

CHRISTIAN DIOR EAU SAVAGE
Where? All good perfume shops and department stores
How much? Prices from £23/$40/€34
Famous for its archetypal 'aftershavey' smell – described by some as 'the very essence of a man' – this was actually the first mass-marketed scent also used by women. Eau Savage was created in 1966, and remains a bestseller. A classic that stands the test of time.

What every gentleman should have in his bathroom cabinet

In the first instance a gentleman should think English. D. R. Harris & Co. (www.drharris.co.uk) of St James's is widely regarded as having the best shaving soap – opt for almond – while Geo. F. Trumper (www.trumpers.com), the Mayfair barbers founded in 1875, has what must be one of the largest selections of razors in the world. For a steady shave try the Warwick, an Edwardian-style razor available with a Gillette Mach-3 blade fitting, which is the best blade.

For the perfect shaving brush, what about one made of pure silver-tip badger from brush experts Kent (www.kentbrushes.com)? Or maybe try Czech & Speake (www.czechspeake.com), or Truefitt & Hill (www.truefittandhill.com). The ultimate shaving oil, which is much more efficient than foam or gel, isn't quite so exclusive. King of Shaves is recommended by all the best barbers, even the most traditional, and is available at all good pharmacies.

Bronzer

St Tropez Shimmering Bronzing Mist

St Tropez
Shimmering
Bronzing
Mist

Where?

www.sttropeztan.com • For stockists call 00 44 115 983 6363

How much?

£32.50/$36/€25

Despite the fact that we're all more wary of sun-exposure than ever before, due to side effects that range from ageing of the skin to melanoma, the desire for a tan refuses to fade. In fact, looking lean and bronzed is a must for modern celebrities and civilians alike. It's best to go to a salon and have fake tan applied by a professional, but if you're short on time and cash, and prepared to do it yourself, the best product you can use is St Tropez's Shimmering Bronzing Mist. This recent innovation comes from the originators of the truly realistic fake tan, and is a consistent favourite with beauty editors and celebs thanks to the three-dimensional sheen, which reflects light and helps make the tan appear deeper and more authentic. It dries quickly, but be warned – you'll need to cover the bathroom floor before applying. This can be a messy little number.

LANCASTER'S INSTANT BRONZE FOAM

Where? www.lancaster-beauty.com • Department stores worldwide

How much? £17.50/$32/€25

Lancaster's Instant Bronze Foam is easy to apply, with a fluffy foamy texture and oil-free consistency. Within a couple of hours it will develop into a long-lasting tan that looks natural and leaves the skin feeling super-soft and smooth.

LANCÔME FLASH BRONZER AIRBRUSH

Where? www.lancome.com • Department stores worldwide

How much? £18/$32/€26

This spray bronzer, raved about by Jessica Simpson and Kylie Minogue, is extremely easy to use: just angle it a few inches from the body and spray away. The very fine mist coats every millimetre of skin and is absorbed easily. Best of all, a natural colour will develop within a couple of hours.

(above) Lancaster's Instant Bronze Foam

(right) Lancôme Flash Bronzer Airbrush

Bubble bath

Laura Mercier Crème Brûlée Honey Bath

Where?
www.lauramercier.com • Department stores worldwide

How much?
£22/$55/€32

Laura Mercier Crème Brûlée Honey Bath

As the poet, Sylvia Plath, once said: 'There must be quite a few things that a bath won't cure, but I don't know many of them.' A long, hot soak is the most indulgent and effective way to unwind after a hard day. Happily, the days when a scoop of bath salts and a bar of cold cream soap would suffice are long gone. Instead, it's now possible to recreate the luxury of a day spa in your own bathroom. A tricky and potentially messy process, but if there's a product that helps you achieve this in one easy step, it's Laura Mercier's Crème Brûlée Honey Bath. With a silky texture and a heavenly, sweet-honey scent that seems good enough to eat, this product creates the finest bubbly bubbles going. Thoroughly luxurious and one of the nicest gifts a girl can give – or receive.

E. COUDRAY JACINTHE AND ROSE BATH CRÈME

Where? L.T. Piver, 152 Rue Gallieni, 92100, Boulogne, France • www.coudray-parfumeur.com • Department stores worldwide

How much? £13/$25/€20

In 1822, during the reign of Louis XVIII, a doctor-chemist named Edmond Coudray started to supply soaps and salves from France to European royalty. Later, this creamy bubble bath became the brand's best-seller. What makes this bubble bath so great is its blancmange-like texture, making it a pleasure to plunge one's hands into before rinsing off under running bathwater. Irresistible.

ROSE & CO. APOTHECARY ROSE PETAL BATH AND SHOWER CRÈME

Where? 84 Main Street, Haworth, West Yorkshire, BD22 8DP • 00 44 1535 646 830 • www.rose-apothecary.co.uk

How much? £8/$14/€11

This gorgeous smelling Yorkshire brand originates from the romantic village of Howarth, once the home of the Brontë sisters and still home to Rose & Co. Apothecary – a shop full of dusty glass cabinets and botanical concoctions. This lavish bubble bath is spiked with pure oil of roses and is mild, gentle and addictively sweet-but-tart. Use it once and you'll be a convert for life.

Rose & Co. Apothecary Rose Petal Bath and Shower Crème

Compact

Givenchy Prisme

Where?
www.givenchy.com • Department stores worldwide
How much?
£22/$39/€32

Givenchy Prisme

One of the most practical, pretty and glamorous make-up items a girl can have, a good compact is a handbag necessity and a quality mirrored style is a prized accessory that will last a lifetime.

Founded by Hubert de Givenchy in 1957, Parfums Givenchy was an instant hit, becoming one of the most desirable beauty brands in the world, thanks, no doubt, to the brand's associations with screen icon of the day, Audrey Hepburn. The French company has maintained its chic image with exquisite offerings, such as the Prisme pressed powder quartet, which allows the user to blend together a perfect shade to match the required skin tone. Available in nine different shades from a beautiful pastel white to 'Impertinent Rose' and 'Cool Beige', its angular, black-lacquer packaging makes it one of the most beautifully designed compacts around.

Chantecaille

CHANTECAILLE
Where? www.chantecaille.com • Department stores worldwide
How much? £40/$71/€58
French-born, US-based Sylvie Chanticaille, the former force behind Prescriptives, has created some of the best foundations and powders in the world. Her finely textured compact make-up powder foundation, presented in a galvanized nickel container, is one of the best compacts on the market. The pale shades are particularly strong and an excellent option for those with fairer skins. Available in eight shades, including shell, camel and peach.

RMK
Where? www.rmkrmk.com
How much? £23/$34/€40
This forward-thinking Japanese brand specializes in pressed powder that has a lovely translucent sparkle and gives a very light and subtly reflective finish. Particularly good on dry or lifeless skins.

RMK Compact

And the best loose powder . . .

With a delicate gold shimmer, **T. Le Clerc's classic Banane Powder** is the legendary loose powder. It was first created in 1881 and is a fine, soft powder that achieves an instant matt finish once applied over foundation. Make-up artists adore the stuff, as does a host of celebrities, including Madonna, Jennifer Aniston and Drew Barrymore.

Face cream

La Prairie Skin Caviar Luxe Cream

Where?
www.laprairie.com
How much?
£210/$315/€308

It's a million-dollar question in a billion-dollar industry – what's the best face cream in the world? Skins vary as much as body shape, hair texture and colouring. There are thousands of creams, ranging from ultra-cheap (see over) to expensive and exclusive emollients to cater for this huge market, so pinpointing just one is practically impossible. According to recent scientific research, venix, the gunky white stuff that covers newborn babies, is apparently the best moisturizer in the world. Eeew. And yes, scientists are working out how they can recreate this and sell it in a jar. But in the meantime, we'll have to make do with good old-fashioned cream moisturizers, and if we had to pick the best all-round effective one, something that glides on beautifully and sinks in without the oil-slick effect, it would have to be La Prairie's Skin Caviar Luxe.

It's not just the expensive-looking blue glass tub and silver spoon that replicates a real caviar spoon – although that's a bonus – or the fact that the Beckhams both use it, this legendary moisturizer actually delivers results. Rich in caviar extract, which is known for its nourishing properties, it is light but rich and sinks in effortlessly. If you could only own one face cream in the world, perhaps this should be it.

Natura Bissé Diamond Cream

La Prairie Skin Caviar Luxe Cream

NATURA BISSÉ DIAMOND CREAM

Where? www.naturabisse.es • Selected department stores worldwide
How much? £150/$270/€220

The silver jar looks expensive and appeals to the inner J-Lo in us all, but it's the cream inside that's valuable. Just one application and you know this is special, as it sinks deeply into the skin. OK, so it doesn't contain diamonds: instead, the potent ingredients are straight from the sea. It's also packed with grapeseed extract, beta-glucans (derived from dried yeast extract), vitamins C and E, and an oligo-collagen complex. Skin is left feeling buffed and polished.

Elemis Pro-Collagen Marine Cream

ELEMIS PRO-COLLAGEN MARINE CREAM

Where? www.elemis.com • Selected salons and department stores worldwide

How much? £75/$135/€110 Crème de La Mer may be the most expensive marine-based face cream in the world – the newest addition, 'Project Precious', contains the rarest ingredients and costs upwards of £1,000 – but the beautifully light Pro-Collagen Marine Cream from Elemis is a much more versatile and affordable option. It is also easier to apply and suits more skin types. Containing the unique *Padina pavonica* algae (a fan-shaped brown algae hand-picked by scuba divers from the temperate waters off Malta), there is also a helping of porphyridum seaweed, chlorella seaweed, mimosa, rose, and gingko biloba. The best way to experience this cream? Have the Elemis Pro-Collagen Japanese Silk Booster Facial, one of the best facials in the world.

Best bargain moisturizers

- **Pond's face cream** (found at most chemists). Originally invented in 1846 as a medicine by scientist Theron T. Pond, who discovered it could heal small wounds, this cream became one of the best selling cosmetic creams of the 20th century and many women, young and old, still swear by it.
- **The Body Shop's Vitamin E Moisture Cream** (www.bodyshop.co.uk). The Body Shop's best-selling product is produced solely from plants and includes antioxidants that protect the skin from the elements. At around £7 ($12), it's also brilliantly affordable.
- **Olay Complete All Day Moisture Lotion** (www.olay.com). A classic fluid moisturiser, now with SPF15, this absorbs into the skin easily. Great for normal skin types.
- **Nivea Creme** (www.nivea.com). Classic Nivea Creme, in its iconic royal blue and white packaging, is the ultimate multifunctional moisturiser as it can be used on the face, body and hands. Good for very dry skins.
- **Weleda Skin Food** (health food shops). A skin-saving natural moisturiser, rich in lanolin and essential oils including lavender and sweet orange, which soothe and nourish very dry skin. Can be used on body and face.

Three of the best organic moisturizers:

- **Dr Hauschka's Quince Day Cream** (www.drhauschka.co.uk) is a hit with Kate Moss and Sadie Frost. A lightweight, natural cream, it contains quince and beeswax extracts, both of which have protective qualities.
- **Jurlique Recover Gel** is a light, vitamin-rich gel that delivers instant refreshing moisturization in one easy application (www.beautyhabit.com).
- **Barefoot Botanicals Rose Fina Intensive Facial Radiance Cream** (www.naturalcollection.com).

Hairbrush

Mason Pearson

Where?
www.sephora.com •
www.hqhair.com • www.escentual.com
All good pharmacies

How much?
Large hairbrush with pure bristle £61/$107/€91

Mason
Pearson

The Mason Pearson hairbrush is a classic and still the best – a bona fide status symbol for the bathroom. Diana, Princess of Wales, always carried a pocket nylon bristle model in her bag, while top hairdressers the world over – think the kind whose names also grace shampoo bottles – recommend this brand to their clientele. Like many great designs, a Mason Pearson brush is all about the details. Part of the reason the brushes work so well is due to a clever pneumatic rubber cushion, which allows the brush to follow the contours of the head and effectively massage the scalp. Mason Pearson, an engineer from Yorkshire, invented the cushion at the height of the Industrial Revolution while working for the British Steam Brush Works. He also invented the handle, specially designed for comfort and originally made of wood. The original style is still available today, although most are now made from plastic that has been carefully hand-polished to remove any sharpened edges.

Brushes come in four sizes: the 'popular large', with six rings of tufts, is suitable for most hair – as a rule of thumb, the longer the hair, the bigger the brush needed. Different hair types require different types of tuft, and Mason Pearson offers three options: natural boar bristle, best for fine to normal hair and less likely to snag the hair than nylon; a mix of nylon and bristle for medium to thick hair and pure nylon – Mason Pearson have developed their own special type of nylon, recommended for very thick hair that tangles. For the folically challenged, there is even a 'sensitive' brush with special bristles that further stimulate scalp circulation.

If cared for correctly, a Mason Pearson brush should last a lifetime. If you have spent hundreds on a haircut and highlights, it has got to be worth it!

KENT NAT20
Where? www.kentbrushes.com • All good pharmacies
How much? £13/$24/€19
The Kent NAT20 porcupine and pure bristle brush with wooden handle is a classic. Kent has been making brushes since 1777 and now makes over 250 models – one of which takes over 540 hours to make, a process that includes drying and hand-finishing the satinwood handle. The Kent dressing table comb also comes highly recommended.

FRÉDÉRIC FEKKAI MINI HAIRBRUSH
Where? Branches of Space NK • www.spacenk.co.uk • www.saksfifthavenue.com • www.sephora.com
How much? £22/$40/€33
This Hollywood superstar hairdresser's brush is nothing short of perfection: handcrafted in France, made from natural boar bristles and tiny enough, not to say chic enough with its tortoiseshell handle, to carry around in your handbag. Perfect for one-upmanship moments in front of a communal bathroom mirror.

Lip balm

Crème de la Mer

Where?
www.cremedelamer.com • Selected department stores worldwide
How much?
£35/$61/€51

The most versatile of all beauty products, lip balm eclipses mascara in terms of its desert island must-have appeal. It is usually the first introduction to make-up a girl has, long before the joys of lipstick and eye shadow are ever allowed, and is adored by make-up artists for its ability to add lustre to cheekbones, eyelids and collarbones. A good lip balm can also smooth scaly elbows, knuckles and knees. But which is the best? Crème de la Mer may be known for producing the most expensive face cream in the world, but it is the lip balm that really shines. The pale-green balm has a lovely sludgy texture, slight minty smell and toffee-tinged taste, but it's the instantly soothing effect on chapped lips that makes it the nicest around. Not so much an everyday lip balm – but then not many of us really need lip balm every day – instead use it to indulge when your lips need some intense moisturising and tender loving care.

Crème de la Mer

SISLEY NUTRITIVE LIP BALM

Where? www.sisley-cosmetics.com • Department stores worldwide
How much? £27/$48/€39

A simple pink-and-white tub holds this rich, waxy lip balm that is great for dried out, cracked lips but also as a day-to-day option. Extremely restorative, Nutritive has been designed to take special care of lips that are chapped or dehydrated by extreme weather conditions. The cocktail of natural plant extracts, including hazelnut oil, sunflower oil, shea and kokum butter, soothe the lips perfectly.

Sisley Nutritive lip balm

KIEHL'S LIP BALM #1

Where? Kiehl's stores worldwide • www.kiehls.com
How much? £6.50/$12/€10

Kiehl's legendary Lip Balm #1, first made in the late 19th century, has been a bestseller at Barneys, Bergdorf Goodman and Fred Segal for decades. It's the quality and sheer simplicity of the product – not to mention that covetable utilitarian packing – that makes it such a hit. The ingredients are all natural – sweet almond oil, vitamin E, aloe vera, wheatgerm oil and vitamin A.

> '*Just like alcohol or cigarettes, some people seem to be more susceptible to becoming dependent.*'
>
> anonymous, www.kevdo.com

Kiehl's Lip Balm #1

Cult lip balms

No other beauty product has such addictive appeal – there's even an American website (www.kevdo.com/lipbalm) to help crack the lip balm habit. **Carmex** surely wins the prize for the most addictive brand. Established in 1937, the company is still family owned. The salve contains alum and salicylic acid, which was originally used to treat cold sores, and, according to kevdo, hits you 'with a rush that rivals crack cocaine when you first apply it'.

Gwyneth Paltrow's favourite is **Smith's Rosebud Salve** – Manhattan's stylish outlet, C.O. Bigelow Apothecaries, sells more than $11,000-worth of this brand every year in mail order alone. The original Rosebud Salve, first prepared in 1892 by a Dr G. F. Smith, boasts a whole host of other uses too – it can be applied to chapped skin, blemishes, nappy rash and detergent burns. **Perfumeria Gal Madrid** is the most decorative lip balm. With its elegant Art Nouveau style packaging, this Spanish salve comes in 10 different colours and scents and is a bestseller across Europe (www.hqhair.com).

Grosella Balm

Carmex Balm

Mascara

Lancôme Definicils

Where?
www.lancome.com • Department stores worldwide
How much?
£17/$25/€20

*Lancôme
Definicils*

*Yves Saint Laurent
Mascara Volume
Effet Faux Cils*

We all know of at least one woman who refuses to leave the house without coating her lashes in mascara. So what's the big deal? Apparently, our obsession roots back to the most basic, primal of reasons – long lashes signify open eyes, good health and alertness, still attractive attributes for encouraging the opposite sex. The trick is to find a mascara that does this naturally, without clogging, smudging, flaking or, worse still, irritating the eyelids. After testing as many as we could possibly get our hands on, we've come out with a clear winner: Lancôme Definicils. It's available in black, brown and the most stylish shade of all, a chic navy that goes with everything and looks good on blondes and brunettes, against black or white skin. It lengthens lashes, doesn't smudge and glides on easily. Without doubt one of the star beauty products of our time.

KANEBO 38°C SILK PERFORMANCE MASCARA
Where? Takashimaya, 693 Fifth Avenue, New York, NY 10022 • 00 1 212 350 0100
How much? £15/$20/€18
Outside Japan, this phenomenal mascara is hard to track down, but you can pick it up at Takashimaya in New York and brand new on eBay. It is worth seeking out because those who use it never go back. It glides on and coats each lash with a special silk case that is guaranteed not to smudge in temperatures below 38°C/100°F, hence the name.

YVES SAINT LAURENT MASCARA VOLUME EFFET FAUX CILS
Where? www.ysl.com • Department stores worldwide
How much? £17/$25/€20
Since launching in 2000, YSL's most popular mascara has been a massive hit thanks to its ability to make the lashes appear instantly glamorous – as if you've just applied the most perfect set of false lashes, in fact.

Best for budget lashes

Maybelline's Great Lash mascara is one of the most overrated products in the world – our testers reported smudging and flaking. Instead, for the best budget options, we recommend **Max Factor's 2000 Calorie mascara** and **Rimmel's Extreme Definition Ultimate Lash Separating mascara**, which features a unique metal wand that is more like a comb than the traditional brush and delivers a perfect application of mascara that lasts all day long.

Nail varnish

OPI Coney Island Cotton Candy

Where?
www.opi.com • Selected salons worldwide
How much?
£8/$14/€12

OPI Coney Island Cotton Candy

If there's one item of make-up that instantly makes the wearer appear ultra-groomed, it's nail polish. The polish you choose speaks volumes. Red can transform a look from plain to vixen, black says punk rock, while pearly pink says Barbie-doll cute. But what's the best? Perhaps a natural shade that looks good with pale skin or a tan, works with a casual day look or a high-octane evening do? OPI, the brand favoured by Cameron Diaz, Kate Hudson and Halle Berry, really is the best of the best. With a great consistency, it glides on nicely and stays on for days. There are a massive 250 colours to choose from with cheeky names like 'I'm Not Really a Waitress' (a striking red) and 'Can't a Berry Have Some Fun?' (a flirty fuchsia pink). The colours you put on are true to the colour you see in the bottle, so you know *exactly* what you're getting.

ESSIE
Where? www.essie.com • Selected salons worldwide
How much? £7.50/$13.50/€11

Essie Weingarten, a beauty industry icon, founded this brand in 1981, driven by her desire for the perfect manicure. Available in a mouthwatering array of colours, Essie's nail polishes feature in all the world's leading spas and salons, including Bliss, Canyon Ranch and La Costa Resort. Popular for their durability and chip resistance, the classic, pretty, neutral shades include Bashful Beige, Pachinko Pale and Ballet Slippers, all of which feature regularly at haute-couture shows. Madonna, Sharon Stone and Julia Roberts are fans.

Essie

REVLON COLORSTAY ALWAYS ON
Where? www.revlon.com • Stores worldwide
How much? £6/$10/€8

With colours that are true to the bottle and often outlast more expensive brands, Revlon glides on easily and lasts for up to a week without chipping. Stay Sheer is a good all-round shade.

Revlon Colorstay Always On

'It is better to apply more thin coats of polish than a few thick coats. The thicker the coat, the longer it takes to dry.'

Leighton Denny, celebrity manicurist

Perfume

Guerlain Shalimar

Guerlain Shalimar

Where?
68 Avenue des Champs Elysées, 75008, Paris, France • 00 33 45 62 52 57 • For other branches and stockists, visit www.guerlain.com

How much?
From £26/$46/€38

A good fragrance – a signature scent – is one that instantly sums up a woman's personality. The ultimate scent, therefore, must be distinctive; it must be relatively hard to get hold of (limited availability is always a pull); it must be French – a country that views perfumery as the most noble of art forms; and it must be a die-hard classic blend, none of that single-noted nonsense that has been popular for the past few years. A flamboyant history also helps. Shalimar from Guerlain, one of France's most prestigious perfume houses, has all of the above.

In the 1920s there was a saying – 'there are three things no respectable woman should do: smoke, dance the tango and wear Shalimar'. When it came out in 1925 the scent was described as 'racy', 'intoxicating' and 'impossibly bewitching'. Its inspiration? An epic love story from India. Three hundred years before, the emperor Shah Jahan built an amazing garden for his favourite wife, calling it Shalimar or 'the temple of love', and filled it with fountains, lakes, marble terraces, rare flowers and plants. But his wife died and Shah Jahan was left broken-hearted, going on to create the most beautiful mausoleum imaginable for his wife: the Taj Mahal.

In keeping with the scent's exotic inspiration, Guerlain concocted what is generally regarded as the world's first 'oriental' scent, a heady mix of bergamot, sandalwood, vetiver, patchouli and vanilla notes, the latter of which is said to have an aphrodisiac effect – no wonder it caused such a sexy stir when it first came out. Then there's the beautiful bottle with the midnight-blue stop, the pride of any dressing table. The design was originally conceived for the Decorative Arts exhibition in Paris, at a time when coloured glass was extremely unusual. The inspiration? Those exotic gardens again, as the shade is said to conjure up images of magical water.

Jean Patou Joy

Unlike many mass-market scents, Shalimar isn't sold everywhere, only at Guerlain's dedicated Parisian boutiques and selected department stores – Bergdorf Goodman in New York, for instance, where it has been a bestseller for more than two decades. At the Guerlain Institut on the Champs Elysées, Paris, Shalimar obsessives can buy supersized bottles, engraved with their own initials.

JEAN PATOU JOY
Where? www.sephora.com • All good department stores
How much? Approximately £48/$88/€70
Joy was launched in 1927 and still retains an air of mystique thanks to its status as 'the world's most expensive perfume' – a moniker that no

longer applies since Clive Christian is now the priciest. It takes over 10,000 jasmine flowers from Grasse in Provence to make a single ounce, the jasmine hand picked at dawn from Patou's own fields for quality-control purposes. Wearers past and present include the Queen and Jackie O.

FRÉDÉRIC MALLE

Frédéric Malle

Where? 37 Rue de Grenelle, 75007, Paris, France • 00 33 1 42 22 77 22 • www.editionsdeparfums.com

How much? From £45/$80/€65

Malle may be new on the scene but he has the right heritage – his grandfather helped develop the fragrance arm of his friend Christian Dior's business – as well as the right attitude, giving some of the world's best noses a free reign to create their own scents. The Paris boutique houses a number of isolation booths, where customers can smell scent in its purest form away from outside pollutants. Already iconic are Lipstick Rose, noted as smelling not unlike a rose and violet bonbon, and Cologne Bigarade, which Chandler Burr, author of *The Emperor of Scent*, describes as, 'the smell of a person in a summer thunderstorm. They are showered and clean, but it is hot, so we can smell their body, neck, clean armpits and the lovely complex smells of the summer clinging to the skin.' Blimey!

Five other cult scents

Recently there's been a revival in cult scents, the kind of fragrances that your granny used to wear and that can be instantly identified from 10 feet away. Most are cult for a reason, usually down to an interesting history and heritage. You know these will never be discontinued.

Chanel No. 5

The world's bestselling scent – there's a bottle sold every 30 seconds. It was launched in 1921 and created hysteria when it first went on sale, as it was seen as personifying Coco, the woman every other woman wanted to be. According to legend, the name exists because Coco rejected the first four.

Nina Ricci L'Air du Temps

Created just after the Second World War – hence the doves of peace adorning every bottle – this scent has a loyal following. It smells feminine and fresh, and started the trend for lighter fragrances.

Rochas Femme

Made in 1944 as an exclusive scent for couturier Marcel Rochas' wife, this is a dry 'chypre' fragrance with a hint of the masculine. The bottle was inspired by the fullness of Mae West's hips.

Ormonde Jayne Frangipani Absolute

Frequently voted one of the best new scents, and made using only the finest frangipani essence – hence the purer-than-pure result. All of Ormonde Jayne's fragrances are created in-house in her London laboratory. Others include unusual ingredients like pink pepper oil and black hemlock.

Caron Tabac Blond

Along with Guerlain, Caron is another classy-yet-clever Parisian perfume house. Tabac Blond was created in 1919 and created quite a stir, thanks to its sandalwoody and somewhat masculine scent, a mix of golden tobacco, tuberose and vanilla. Utterly distinctive – a fragrance some women go batty about.

Red lipstick

Yves Saint Laurent Rouge Pur # 20

Where?
www.ysl.com • Department stores worldwide
How much?
£15.50/$28/€23

The ancient Egyptians were the first to be seduced by the power of red lips. They used henna to paint theirs, a look that signifies strength. Red lipstick still instills fear in some because they imagine they will end up looking like a freaky clown. Truth is, while not all reds suit everyone – and there are literally thousands of variations from flirty pink reds to siren scarlets – there are some shades – true reds, neither blue-toned, nor yellow tinged – that suit pretty much any colouring, from pale Scandinavian complexions to olivey Mediterranean shades. Your lipstick does not need to match your outfit, but it does need to match your complexion. Classic English roses look good with most reds as the tone of the skin complements a true red and a pink red. Those with golden complexions look better in warm (yellowy) reds, while blue reds can clash a little with a warm skin-tone. A modern classic, this vibrant true red-red from YSL delivers the perfect hit of colour, suiting most who try it. The real beauty of this product, apart from the angular packaging emblazoned with the stylish YSL logo, is that it can be worn with ease on a glamorous night out, in the boardroom or to lunch. Don't leave the house without it.

'I'm obsessed with red lips. If you don't wear lipstick, I can't talk to you. You need to have lips – they're very important for getting men.'
Isabella Blow, fashion designer

'My all time favourite red lipstick is the one my mother wore. I always begged her for a dab whenever she put it on. I've no idea who it was by, but it came in a heavy gold case and smelled to me of pure glamour. My modern equivalent is Chanel's Rouge Star – I've worn it since the 1980s and I always go back to it whenever I need a fix of red lipstick.'
Anna-Marie Solowij, Beauty Director, British Vogue

Yves Saint Laurent Rouge Pur #20

Guerlain's Kiss Kiss Exces de Rouge #523

Givenchy Lip Lip Lip! Shopping Red #212

GUERLAIN'S KISS KISS EXCES DE ROUGE #523

Where? www.guerlain.co.uk • Department stores worldwide
How much? £15/$27/€21
The gold packaging will make this one of the most attractive items in your make-up bag. Plus, the punchy pillar-box shade is one of the most versatile around.

GIVENCHY LIP LIP LIP! SHOPPING RED #212

Where? www.givenchy.com • Department stores worldwide
How much? £14/$25/€20
Sleek packaging and a smooth, glide-on texture make this bold, bright red an indulgent option.

Other top reds to suit all skin shades

- **Chanel Fire #65**: A bold, true red.
- **Dior Rouge Mysore #763**: A striking, pinky red.
- **Nars Jungle Red**: A bright, modern red.
- **MAC Russian Red**: A sexy, starlet red.
- **Estée Lauder #725**: A rich, intense red.
- **Laura Mercier Seduction**: A sexy red.
- **Bourjois Rouge Best #15**: A deep, sultry red.

Soap

Savon de Marseille

Where?

La Compagnie de Provence, 1 Rue Caisserie, 13001, Marseille, France • 00 33 4 91 56 20 94 • www.thefrenchhouse.net

How much?

Approximately £2/$3.50/€2.80 per block

Savon de Marseille

We're talking hand soap here, so it needs to look good on your washbasin, not as if you've been squirreling away freebies from hotels. It also needs to smell great – and work! Luckily, Savon de Marseille fits the bill on every count.

Many French women believe Savon de Marseille has magical properties, thanks to the way it is made. Indeed, Marseille has a long tradition of soap making. Its soap is made from oil, alkali from sea plants, seawater – and nothing else. No additives, no artificial colours, no animal fats, nothing. The green bars, which are scent-free, are made with olive oil, the white/beige with palm oil. Each block is stamped with the legend 'extra pur 72% d'huile garanti', a standard since 1688.

Marseille's remaining *savonneries* still use the same centuries-old method to make soap. First they brew the ingredients in cauldrons for at least ten days, rinsing repeatedly to remove any excess soda. Each block is then cut by hand – producing a satisfyingly rustic result – and left to dry naturally on racks, a process that can take months. The soap is sold by weight and each block lasts for ages. Incidentally, soap in general is currently enjoying a renaissance simply because it doesn't contain the chemicals found in some shower gels.

AFRICAN BLACK SHEA BUTTER SOAP

Where? www.akamuti.co.uk

How much? £3.50/$6.50/€5 per bar

There are lots of shea butter imitators out there but Akamuti sells the real deal. Shea butter comes from the nuts of the karite tree, which grows wild in Africa and can't be cultivated. The production process is complicated, laborious and local; Akamuti is a Fairtrade company, so proceeds go towards helping the surrounding community. Black shea butter soap contains no preservatives or additives and aids dry skin, dermatitis and sunburn. It is also excellent for eczema – many longterm sufferers swear by it.

CLAUS PORTO SABONETE AROMATICO

Where? www.clausporto.com • www.spacenk.co.uk • www.thesoapbar.com • All good Portuguese pharmacies

How much? Approximately £8/$15/€12

The Portuguese and Spanish are fanatical about soap, especially bars that come prettily wrapped and gorgeously scented. Claus Porto's creamy products, handmade in Portugal since 1887, fit the bill perfectly, and include exciting scents like Pear Sandalwood and Red Poppy. Great for gifts.

Home

'Have nothing in your homes that you do not know to be useful or believe to be beautiful.'

William Morris, designer, 1834–96

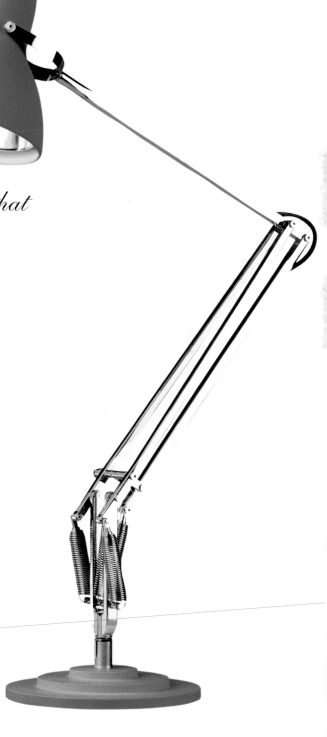

Alarm clock

Jacob Jensen

Where?
www.jacob-jensen.com •
Various outlets, including: www.designmuseumshop.org

How much?
£33/$60/€48

Jacob Jensen

An alarm clock is the first thing you see every morning, so it had better look good. The Danish designer, Jacob Jensen, excels in making ordinary objects – telephones and doorbells – look extraordinary. He first came to prominence as the chief designer for Bang & Olufsen, the upmarket hi-fi brand, working with them for almost 30 years, and designing more than 80 different products, before branching out on his own. Jensen is now credited with enabling us to view everyday objects with a designer's eye. It is little wonder, then, that he is represented in a number of museums around the world, among them New York's Museum of Modern Art, where he has 19 products in the Design Collection and Design Study Collection.

Jensen's alarm clock was launched in 1999. Like many of his products, the clock is characterized by its sleek lines and subdued metal colouring, and has received the prestigious Red Dot award for industrial design. It looks simple, unobtrusive, and just a little bit *Star Wars*, not to say aesthetically pleasing: the LCD used to display the time has been inversed to make it look more attractive – and less obtrusive for sleepy eyes. The clock is also easy to use – it has just four keys, the concept being that one key equals one function. And for the truly lazy, a similar model is radio-controlled.

Intrepid clock connoisseurs should also head to Japan, land of the all singing, all dancing, voice-responsive mini-robotic alarm clock. The Akihabara area in Tokyo heaves under the weight of the latest in wacky wake-up technology – at surprisingly reasonable prices.

BRAUN TRAVEL ALARM CLOCK
Where? www.goodmans.net • Good electronics stores
How much? £25/$45/€36
This is lo-fi Bananarama-era utilitarian chic at its best for those who don't want digital – and, more importantly, want something that ticks. Fans include Los Angeles-based interior designer Brad Dunning, who puts this matt black clock at the bedside of 'almost every client' – think Tom Ford and Sofia Coppola.

LUMIE BODYCLOCK
Where? www.lumie.com • Most large department stores, including: www.johnlewis.com
How much? From £60/$108/€87
This ingenious new invention regulates the user's melatonin cycle and sleeping pattern by stimulating dawn with a gradually intensifying light. Olympic rowing champion Ed Coode took one to the last games – and just think how early rowers rise.

Bed

DUX 7007

Where?
www.duxbed.com

How much?
Single (plus mattress)
£2,705(£439)/$4,745($771)/
€4,016(€652)

DUX 7007 Bed

The ultimate modern-day luxury? Getting a good night's sleep, one precious commodity that nowadays money *can* actually buy – albeit at a price. Duxiana make what has to be the ultimate bed, a combination of scientifically researched and tested mattresses – including extra springs that enable the mattress to conform to the sleeper's body shape, great when two people who prefer mattresses of differing firmnesses share a bed – with traditional wooden fittings. The Swedish company, established in 1926, crafts the kind of beds that are passed down from generation to generation, such is their durability. One of the many hi-tech details is a headboard made from northern Swedish pine, where the cold winters create super-strength wood, with controls that can be adjusted to provide support when reading. The DUX 7007 model was recently voted the best bed in the *Wallpaper** Design Awards – making the design the acceptable face of divans!

What's more, according to independent research, DUX beds are the best for inducing deep sleep, the stage necessary for proper bodily recuperation. The study noted that sleepers on a DUX bed entered the deep sleep phase faster and stayed in the state longer than they did using other beds. So it would seem that to get more sleep you really must spend more cash.

SIMON HORN SOLID EUROPEAN WALNUT LIT BATEAU

Where? www.simonhorn.com
How much? From £2,445/$4,291/€3,630
Also known as a 'sleigh bed', this particular style has won a stack of design awards. Simon Horn, a former City broker based in London, is widely credited with kick-starting the renaissance of the French bed. All of his models are built by hand and are said to improve with age. Such is his cachet that Angelina Jolie bought a Simon Horn cherrywood crib for her baby, Zahara.

LOUIS XVI ANTIQUE BED

Where? Antique shops, especially those specializing in French furniture, including:
www.judygreenwoodantiques.co.uk • www.pughs-antiques-export.com • www.atlamaison.com
How much? From £650/$1,141/€965
Beds don't come more rococo than this, with its signature flourishes on the curved head and footboards. Karl Lagerfeld is said to sleep on a particularly ostentatious version embellished with royal blue velvet and gold tassels – the ultimate boudoir furniture.

Bed linen

Pratesi

Where?

829 Madison Avenue at 69th Street, New York, NY 10021 • 00 212 288 2315 • www.pratesi.com

How much?

A basic 480-thread-count sheet starts at £825/$1,420/€2,063

Pratesi bed linen

Enveloping oneself in crisp, white bed linen is undoubtedly the nicest way to sleep. Pratesi is synonymous with expensive bedclothes, considered by many thread-count obsessives (a thread-count is the number of threads in a one-inch square of fabric, and some of Pratesi's are well over 700) as superior to the more ubiquitous Frette. Treated properly, good bed linen is an investment that will last a lifetime – and, since we spend on average a third of our lives in bed, is definitely worth paying for. Stick to plain white or white with discreet embroidery – the 'Three Lines' embroidered Pratesi range, is striking yet simple and won't date.

Pratesi is an Italian family-run company that has been going for five generations and the manufacturing of each sheet adheres to strict rules. All embroidery is done by hand, for instance, and all apprentices are taught for a minimum of five years before they're allowed to start work on any linen. But it's not just the thread count that, well, counts - of equal importance is the provenance of the cotton, the best coming from Egypt where the yarn actually gets softer and smoother with time and wear. Pratesi are super-picky and use only the top 0.002 per cent.

As sheet snobs will readily attest, getting obsessed with bedding is an expensive habit and, after sleeping on a high thread-count, anything else feels like sandpaper. It's little wonder, then, that according to one Pratesi representative: 'Our hardest sell is the first-time customer. Once they buy Pratesi, they're our customers forever'.

FRETTE COTTON-SATIN EGYPTIAN SHEETS
Where? Montenapoleone, 21 Milan, Italy • 00 39 278 39 50 • www.frette.com
How much? From about £255/$450/€370 per sheet
The company was founded by Edmond Frette in the French city of Grenoble in 1860. It soon moved over the border to Italy, where it swiftly established itself as the official supplier to the Italian royal family, as well as the Vatican. Frette's collections offer sheets with interesting borders and crocheted lace insets.

D. PORTHAULT
Where? 18 Avenue Montaigne, 75008, Paris, France • 00 33 1 47 20 75 25 • 18 East 69th Street, New York, NY 10021 • 00 1 212 688 1660
How much? From £342/$600/€507
Truman Capote once said that the difference between the rich and the rest of us was super-fresh vegetables and crisp Porthault sheets. The company was founded in 1925, when Madeline Porthault decided to introduce colour and patterns to a world of linen that was previously pure white. The label was a favourite of both Jackie and JFK and the Duke and Duchess of Windsor – both couples slept on monogrammed Porthault sets.

Blanket

Vintage Welsh wool blanket

Where?
Labour and Wait, 18 Cheshire Street, London E2
• 00 44 207 729 6253 • www.labourandwait.co.uk
How much?
Prices from £65/$144/€96

Welsh wool blanket from Labour and Wait

OK, so the absolute ultimate may be a Hermès cashmere blanket, which costs a couple of thousand pounds and is what Kate Moss, ever the style expert, has decreed her desert island essential. But that's simply not realistic.

No, the best blankets actually come from Wales. These are not nearly as soft as cashmere, but what Welsh blankets lack in pleasing tactility, they more than make up for in durability. Traditional Welsh blankets are more subtle in colour than their Scottish counterparts – the vegetable dyes used produce a softer hue – but they are just as robust, not to say exceptionally warm. Indeed, it is said that Welsh sheep have especially rough fleeces to combat all that rain.

Wales had a thriving weaving industry until the end of the Second World War, when it could no longer compete with the bigger mills of England. The most covetable Welsh blankets, therefore, are the pre-1940s examples. Once found in every Welsh bedroom – the best are double-weave – they are, alas, not quite so easy to track down now, as a number of collectors have got in on the act, not to say certain designers like Ralph Lauren, who has been known to buy up old blankets and draw inspiration from their colourways.

To avoid disappointment, head to Labour and Wait, a cultish London hardware store located along a tiny East End street. The shop specializes in what it describes as 'timeless, functional products', the kind of simple goods that are nowadays almost impossible to find, such as enamel milk pans and balls of twine. The couple who own the shop have simple good taste and an eye for detail, and since they spend months scouring the world for the best of the best, you can be sure that the vintage Welsh blankets on sale here will be better than any you'd find in the Welsh Valleys today. Buy one with detachable leather straps – perfect for picnics when the weather gets warmer. That way you'll be using your blanket all year round.

Peruvian Alpaca blanket

PERUVIAN ALPACA BLANKET
Where? Andean handicraft markets, such as Chinchero and Pisac
How much? Approximately £11/$20/€16
Alpaca, the fleece of llama-like creatures raised in the Andes, is five times warmer than sheep's wool. The best Alpaca buys are found in Peru itself, but shop carefully, as the animal oils on the fibres can leave some blankets smelly.

THE WHITE COMPANY
Where? 8 Symons Street, London, SW3, and branches • 00 44 207 823 5322 • www.thewhitecompany.com
How much? £595/$1,073/€882
Admittedly cashmere doesn't wear as well as wool, especially in blanket form, but The White Company's reversible cashmere blanket with a satin trim is much cheaper than the Hermès version – and you can't beat the luxe-factor.

Candle

Diptyque

Where?

34 Boulevard Saint Germain, 75005, Paris, France • 00 33 1 43 26 45 27 •
www.diptyqueparis.com

How much?

£29.50/$52/€42

Once upon a time there was potpourri – and that was it. *And* it didn't smell particularly potent. In the past few years, however, selecting the aroma of one's home has become almost as important as selecting your own signature scent, thanks in part to the worldwide trend towards cocooning. Add to that the fact that smell is the most powerful of the senses and you have a mini-revolution on your hands.

Diptyque is king of the candles. Its little glass containers, with their distinctive black-and-white typography, mark out a smart home, while a whiff of their scents is instantly recognizable – unlike many candles, Diptyque's contain a high percentage of natural oils and essences.

The brand has long been popular with the fashion crowd – Phoebe Philo likes Pomander, while Karl Lagerfeld burns Cannelle and Héliotrope together. John Galliano, another loyal customer, has even worked with the company to produce his own scent; described as a 'warm, deep and dense fragrance with no flowers at all', it is one of the strongest smelling in the range.

The Diptyque scent that smells the most heavenly is the hot topic of many a beauty site's chatroom. Although popularity is somewhat seasonal – shoppers prefer spicier scents, such as Pomander (cinnamon and orange) and Feu de Bois (firewood) in the run-up to Christmas – the overall bestsellers remain Figuier (fig tree), Tubereuse (tuberose) and, at the absolute top, Baies, a combination of blackcurrant and Bulgarian rose. Such is Baies' cult status that it was the only scent chosen to be converted into a limited-edition black candle to mark Diptyque's 40-year anniversary, and die-hard, won't-burn-any-other-fragrance fans include Natalie Portman, Kylie Minogue and the supermodel Natalia Vodianova.

For the ultimate Diptyque experience, visit the original wood-panelled Saint Germain store, the address of which is etched on every bottle. Here, experienced sales staff will uncover each jar and encourage you to inhale deeply. Indeed, until as recently as 1999, this is where all the big department stores had to collect their orders from – and

Lauren Bacall would actually make an annual Christmas pilgrimage to Paris simply to collect her seasonal scents.

If you still hanker for pot pourri, though, the best can be bought from the Florence-based pharmacy Santa Maria Novella, at Via della Scala 16, near the church of the same name.

Diptyque Baies

VOTIVO NO. 96
Where? www.scentsandsprays.com • Department stores and boutiques around the world
How much? £25/$20/€35
The Red Currant edition, favourite of many a fragrant shopkeeper, has a distinctive berry scent that is pleasingly potent. Treated with care, this candle will burn for 50 hours.

NATURAL MAGIC
Where? www.naturalmagicuk.com
How much? £32.50/$57/€48
Just when you thought a scented candle couldn't be in the least bit harmful, scientists discover that paraffin produces carcinogenic fumes that can be as perilous as passive smoking. Candles from Natural Magic, however, are made from vegetable wax, leaving your lungs – and walls – soot-free, plus the oils are 100 per cent organic. They smell fab, too; no wonder Sienna Miller and Liz Hurley are fans.

Chair

Barcelona chair, No. MR90

Where?

Aram • 110 Drury Lane, London, WC2 • 00 44 207 557 7557 • www.aram.co.uk • Knoll, Inc. 76 9th Avenue, Floor 11, New York, NY 10011 • 001 212 343 4000 • www.knoll.com

How much?

From £3,165/$5,660/€4,611 for basic black

Because it's the most practical and used piece of furniture, designers have always viewed the chair as an object through which they can make a statement about their design philosophy. In 1929, the German designer, Ludwig Mies van der Rohe, made a chair for the Spanish king, Alfonso XIII, and his queen. It was fashioned in luxurious white leather with a steel frame and looked strikingly contemporary but thoroughly regal too. To this day it remains one of the most desirable chairs of all time, perhaps because it has an almost throne-like quality – it is as opulent as it is modern. Originals, dating back to before the Second World War, fetch around £10,000 each – at least three times more than later versions – and can be identified by their bent, chrome top-rail and feet with a more pronounced curve. Now reissued in a slightly simpler form and structure, with its modern but deeply masculine and luxurious shape, the Barcelona chair remains one of the most desirable pieces of furniture you can buy – the perfect combination of style and function.

Barcelona chair, No. MR90

LOUNGE CHAIR, BY CHARLES & RAY EAMES, 1956

Where? Vitra Ltd, 30 Clerkenwell Road, London, EC1 • 00 44 207 608 6200 • www.vitra.com

How much? From £4,125/$7,309/€6,032 for chair and ottoman

Charles and Ray Eames fused contemporary aesthetic with ergonomic theory to create furniture that combined the utmost comfort with high-end materials. Created in 1956, the Lounge Chair is a modern interpretation of the traditional club chair, and is now a classic in the history of modern furniture. Finished in rosewood, faced with moulded plywood and with sumptuous leather seats, it still reeks of boardroom power and style.

MARCEL BREUER WASSILY CHAIR

Where? TwentyTwentyOne, 274 Upper Street, London, N1 • 00 44 207 288 1996 • www.twentytwentyone.com

How much? From £682/$1,197/€1,012

In 1925, the German architect Marcel Breuer began experimenting with tubular steel after being inspired by his trusty Adler bicycle. The outcome was the B3, which became known as the Wassily. Its cubic proportions and the contrast between the fluidity of the steel and tautness of the canvas – Breuer was part of the Bauhaus movement – mean that more than 80 years after its invention, it remains one of the most contemporary chairs on the market.

Jacobsen's 3107 Ant Chair

Breuer's Wassily Chair

Eames Lounge Chair and Ottoman

Chandelier

Swarovski

Where?
137 Regent Street, London, W1 • 00 44
207 434 2500 •
www.swarovskisparkles.com

How much?
Prices on application

Unashamedly opulent, hugely extravagant, and just a little bit bling, the chandelier has recently made it back into fashion thanks to a new generation of forward-thinking innovators, from Tord Boontje to Tom Dixon, offering new possibilities. Sure, the original and most ornate still originate from the France of Louis XV and Louis XVI, Eastern Europe and Russia, but there's now a whole new generation of startling, sparkling chandeliers to adorn contemporary interiors. The modern chandelier is akin to dazzling jewellery for the ceiling and is not just reserved for ballrooms and boardrooms these days.

Daniel Swarovski founded the eponymous brand in 1892 after inventing an industrial device for cutting crystal jewellery stones with precision. Swarovski crystal has since adorned icons such as Marlene Dietrich, and Marilyn Monroe famously wore a gown sparkling with more than 10,000 Swarovski crystals to John F. Kennedy's birthday party in 1962 – it later sold for £556,000/$1 million. Today Swarovski chandeliers

Tom Dixon's Swarovski Chandelier

adorn New York's Metropolitan Opera House, the Chateau of Versailles and the Kremlin in Moscow. Daniel's great granddaughter, Nadja Swarovski, has recently injected new life and excitement into the brand by commissioning some of the world's most renowned designers to create new and spectacular interpretations on the chandelier, including Andrée Putman, Tom Dixon, Solange Azagury-Partridge, Tord Boontje and Yves Béhar.

HARAKATI
Where? 00 44 207 820 8522 • info@harakati.com • Liberty, Regent's Street, London W1 • 00 44 207 734 1234
How much? £300/$528/€443
The Samba light by this talented Japanese designer is an eye-catching, beaded, drop chandelier that makes an elegant, modern and affordable centrepiece for the modern interior.

KUMULUS
Where? Richard Chin • 00 44 1386 47990 • www.bsweden.com
How much? Private commissions from £5,522/$9,718/€8,152
A striking and intricate modern design by Peter Nilsson for BSweden, this light will instantly become the focal point of any room it's put in.

China

Thomas Goode

Where?

19 South Audley Street, Mayfair, London, W1 •
00 44 207 499 2823 •
www.thomasgoode.com

How much?

From £65/$114/€96 for a bespoke plate

Dating back to 1800 and originally devised by Josiah Spode, fine bone china is a more delicate and prized alternative to porcelain. It is also the ultimate tool for keeping up with the Jones' – show it off by displaying it on dressers, in cabinets, on worktops and in kitchen cupboards for maximum effect. And if you really want to outdo the couple at number 35, start buying Thomas Goode. The British company was

Thomas Goode fine bone china

established in 1827 and has a history of supplying china to international royalty, that includes over 32 different commissions for the current British royal family alone. To this day, the small, dedicated team of craftsmen take bespoke orders and can incorporate family monograms, logos, type or even a coat of arms onto their bone china plates. Thomas Goode has also recently collaborated with Versace and Paul Smith.

Wedgwood plate & bowl

WEDGWOOD

Where? 158 Regent Street London, W1 • 00 44 207 734 7262 • www.wedgwood.com

How much? Plates from about £10/$17.50/€14.75

Coined the 'Father of English Potters', Josiah Wedgwood founded his own pottery company in 1759 in the village of Etruria that soon became one of the most respected and revered producers of bone china and ceramics in Europe. Wedgwood has recently revamped its image, utilizing the brand's unique and rich heritage, most notably through the

Wedgwood cup and saucer

Robert Dawson collection, which appropriates the classic willow pattern design, enlarging and distorting it so that it looks vibrant and modern. The company has also collaborated with Jasper Conran. The delightful Harlequin range revives old-fashioned patterns and details and, best of all, arrives in delectable packaging with classic designs depicting the signature Wedgwood cameos.

ROYAL DOULTON

Where? www.royaldoulton.com
How much? Cup and saucer from £20/$35/€29
This classic English brand was established in Stoke-on-Trent, Staffordshire, in 1815. Famed for its collectable china figurines, Royal Doulton is also known for its traditional fine china dinnerware and has recently started collaborating with designers including Zandra Rhodes.

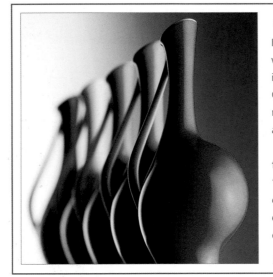

The best antique china

In 1710, Meissen of Germany (www.meissen.com) became the world's first porcelain-producing factory. This porcelain can be identified by its blue sword stamp, and was sold mainly from Germany's famous china centre, Dresden, where an artistic movement encompassing art, culture, poetry, painting, philosophy – and, most importantly, china – flourished.

Spode, England's oldest pottery company, was one of the first factories to use bone china. Spode is most famous for its classic 'Blue Italian' range (www.spode.co.uk), but any of its china is highly covetable, as is the chic German brand Rosenthal. Originally established in 1879, Rosenthal continues to produce chic and elegant bone china (www.int.rosenthal.de).

Left: Rosenthal Pregnant Luise vases

HOW TO SET A TABLE

- A table should always be laid in advance of your guests' arrival.
- You should either lay a table cloth or, if you want to show off the table, then place mats are a necessity.
- Forks should always be placed on the left of the setting with tines (prongs) facing up, while the knife with blade facing inwards) should be placed to the right of the setting, along with any spoons that are needed.
- Spoons should only be placed above the plate when you are short on space.
- Side plates should always be placed to the left.
- Napkins should be folded simply and laid on the side plate.
- Glasses should be laid just above the knife and there should be a different wine glass for each type of wine served, plus a separate glass for water.

Cigars

Partagas Reserva Serie D No 4.

Where?

Davidoff, 35 St James's Street, London, SW1 • 00 44 207 930 3079 • www.davidoff.com • Hunters & Frankau • 00 44 207 471 8400 • www.cigars.co.uk

How much?

A box of 25 costs £278/$488/€413

The best cigars are hand-rolled Cuban numbers, known in the trade as 'Havanas'. Cuban cigars are so good because the country's soil and climate is ideal for growing tobacco, and, rather like a fine wine, age brings out their flavour. Havana houses a number of world-renowned cigar manufacturers, including Cohiba, Montecristo and Partagas, one of the oldest, which makes cigars in much the same way it did when the factory opened in the 1840s.

One thing that *has* changed, though, is the 'reserva'. Launched early in 2005, reserva is predicted to add a new layer of luxury to the world of handmade cigars. Reserva refers to specially selected tobacco leaves that have been fermented for longer – as long as five years, in fact; a single year is much more usual. So already they're more flavoursome than most. Add to that the fact that the binder, the substance that holds together the filler made up of leaves, and the wrapper have also been aged for five years and, well, you have something rather special.

The best brands – Montecristo, Cohiba, Partagas – have all got their hands on reserva cigars, each limited to 5,000 numbered boxes. Partagas' Reserva 'torpedo' cigars, which are tapered at the end, have been introduced as part of Serie D, already a renowned line.

Not only do these cigars taste fantastic, they also make a wise investment. Christie's holds twice-yearly cigar auctions – those from before the 1963 Cuban embargo are especially coveted – so if connoisseurs are going crazy for the Partagas Reserva now, imagine what they'll be doing in 20 years time. Investment cigars should be stored correctly – many suppliers also offer special storage facilities.

Partagas Reserva Serie D No 4.

COHIBA DOUBLE CORONA

Where? J.J. Fox & Robert Lewis, 19 St James's Street, London, SW1 • 00 44 207 930 3787 • www.jjfox.co.uk

How much? £48/$85/€70 per cigar.

This is the most expensive cigar offered by esteemed cigar sellers Fox's. Impossibly smooth and sophisticated, many aficionados claim this is the best cigar they have ever smoked.

VINTAGE DUNHILLS AND DAVIDOFFS

Where? www.cgarsltd.co.uk

How much? For 25 Davidoff Chateau Y'Quem: £5,000/$8,824/€7,300

Dunhills and Davidoffs made before 1992 – in other words, when they were still being made in Cuba – are particularly prized. The ultimate? Davidoff Chateau Y'Quem. In the cigar world, incidentally, anything pre-1995 is vintage.

Coffee maker

Gaggia Titanium

Where?

www.gaggia.com • Good department stores worldwide

How much?

£725/$1,296/€1,056

For the true coffee connoisseur, a good-quality coffee maker is an absolute must. There are hundreds of contraptions, including percolators, vacuum pots and fully automatic machines that administer this most potent of legal stimulants, but which comes top of the list? We found many that performed well, including Swedish brand Jura and US brand Krups, but we have honed them down to the three mentioned here, which between them include the best fully automated, the most good-looking and the most iconic.

The first espresso machine was patented in 1901 by an Italian named Luigi Bezzera, but the concept of forcing hot water through a filter of ground coffee beans wasn't developed until the late 1930s. Achilles Gaggia's purpose-built espresso machine, with a piston and lever system, was introduced in 1946 and was widely seen in 1950s coffee bars throughout Europe, so it's no surprise that one of the most superior espresso machines on the market is by this experienced brand. Just press a button and the beans are ground and the coffee measured and brewed into the cup. It looks good too – in sleek stainless steel with a built-in warmer, automatic milk-frother and electronically programmable portion control.

Gaggia Titanium

ILLY X1 FRANCIS ESPRESSO MACHINE

Where? www.illyusa.com
How much? £444/$800/€652

A favourite with TV and film directors because of its classic good looks, this stylish creation is manufactured by Illy, the first company to create an automatic coffee machine in 1935. With its retro styling, the Illy – designed by Italian architect Luca Trazzi – includes a pump to maintain the ideal pressure for coffee extraction, strong steam pressure for frothing milk and a brewing handle for ground coffee.

Illy X1 Francis espresso machine

LA PAVONI 'PROFESSIONAL'

Where? Via Privata Gorlzia 7, 20098, Milan • 00 39 02 98 21 71 • www.lapavoni.com • Department stores worldwide
How much? £302/$529/€439

It's not automatic and requires a little more patience and expertise to use, but this lovely looking espresso maker from La Pavoni – a company that was founded by Desiderio Pavoni in Milan in 1903 and is credited with inventing the espresso machine – is surely one of the most loveable and classic designs that ever adorned a kitchen.

La Pavoni 'professional'

> **'** *I have measured out my life with coffee spoons.'*
>
> T.S. Eliot, poet

KNOW YOUR COFFEE

- **Americano or lungho**: Coffee made from espresso with hot water.
- **Coretto**: An espresso with alcohol in it.
- **Crema**: That velvety thick top layer of coffee.
- **Espresso**: Literally, 'of the moment', this is the base of all good coffee. The standard shot for an espresso is 7g (⅙oz) of coffee.
- **Cappucino**: Espresso with frothy milk on the top.
- **Ristretto**: A stronger, even smaller espresso.
- **Tamping**: The process of compressing the ground coffee before the water filters through it.

COFFEE FACTS

- Coffee was discovered in AD 850 by an Ethiopian goat herder who noticed his goats were friskier after eating the berries from coffee bushes.
- The world's first coffee house opened in Constantinople in 1475. It wasn't until 1652 that one opened in London.
- 57 countries produce coffee in more than 100 growing regions worldwide, including Brazil, Columbia and Kenya.
- 400 billion cups of coffee are consumed annually worldwide, which means it is the world's second most sought after commodity after oil.

Coffee table

Eileen Gray E1027

Where?
Aram, 110 Drury Lane, WC2 • 00 44
207 557 7557 • www.aram.co.uk
How much?
£363/$649/€525

Eileen Gray E1027 adjustable side table

While at first glance it seems functional and ordinary, look a little closer and the subtle sophistication of this adjustable occasional table begins to shine through. Check the tinted glass top and smooth curves of the frame – sterile, stark and functional. The celebrated architect and designer, Eileen Gray, developed this timeless and modern occasional table in the 1920s, naming it after her cubist flat-roofed house on the French Cote d'Azur. And while it is not the most expensive, spectacular or decadent of tables, it is in its own quiet way the ultimate design classic, which is why it can be found in the Museum of Modern Art's permanent collection. The joy of the E1027 is that it can fit into practically any context, from a modern warehouse apartment to a small Victorian living room.

'*Eileen Gray's E1027 table is among the best known examples of early 20th-century furniture design, and like all great examples of design, is both elegant and practical. When she designed the table in the late 1920s, Gray was looking forward to her sister coming to visit and, knowing that she loved breakfast in bed, designed a compact circular table specifically for that purpose.*'

Alice Rawsthorn, Design Commentator

NOAS PAPION
Where? Aram, 110 Drury Lane, WC2 • 00 44 207 557 7557 • www.aram.co.uk
How much? £363/$649/€525
This sleek, space-age, double-layered, glass coffee table, which featured in the most recent *Star Wars* movie, has two adjustable surfaces.

Noas Papion

ANTONIO CITTERIO EILEEN
Where? B&B Italia, 250 Brompton Road, SW3 • 00 44 207 591 8111 • www.bebitalia.it • Stores throughout Europe
How much? From £440/$787/€636
A homage to Eileen Gray's classic E1027 table, this contemporary style features sleek steel bases and coloured frames.

Cutlery

David Mellor Pride

Where?
4 Sloane Square, London, SW1 • 00 44 207 730 4259
• www.davidmellordesign.com
How much?
From about £1,000/$1,823/€1,484

David Mellor Pride

Utilitarian though it is, good quality cutlery, also known as flatware, enhances the look of a dining room and can impress dinner guests no end. The ultimate cutlery should be sleek, streamlined and silver. You want the fork to feel good to the touch, the knife to be a joy to cut with, and the handle of the spoon to fit snugly into the ball of your hand as you scoop up that last piece of apple pie and custard. David Mellor's classic 1950s-style cutlery is a fabulous investment because it has all the right credentials – elegant, sleek and smooth and an utter pleasure to use. His sets are highly collectable too. Sheffield-born Mellor trained as a silversmith in his teens. Drawing on the historic traditions of Sheffield cutlery, he was inspired to design the Pride range while studying at the Royal College of Art in London. It went into production in 1953, winning one of the earliest Design Centre Awards in 1957. Still manufactured in David Mellor's factory, the Round Building in Derbyshire, it has been in continuous production for over 50 years and is generally acknowledged as one of the most iconic 20th-century modernist designs. Found in stylish homes and museums across the world.

Villeroy & Boch Sereno

PUIFORCAT
Where? 48, Avenue Gabriel, 75008, Paris, France • 00 33 1 45 63 10 10 • www.porcelaingalleryinc.com
How much? Five place service £1,255/$2,270/€1,835
Founded by Jean Puiforcat in 1820, this elite French silversmith handcrafts cutlery to precise specifications. The silver collection spans centuries of design, from ornate and traditional French patterns to clean-lined contemporary masterpieces. The brand has recently created the elegant three-pronged fork, found in the modern Annecy range.

VILLEROY & BOCH SERENO
Where? 33 Duke of York Square, London, SW3 • 00 44 207 730 6527 • www.villeroy-boch.com
How much? 44 pieces from £485/$874/€711
Perfect streamlined proportions ensure that the Sereno range remains desirable. The French brand harks back to 1748 when François Boch established a ceramic tableware business in the French village of Audun-le-Tiche. His business went on to be instrumental in the 1930s' Bauhaus movement.

Desk lamp

Anglepoise

Where?
www.anglepoise.com
How much?
From £69.50/$122/€102

It is maybe not the most spectacular of desk lamps, but the Anglepoise is the most instantly recognizable and iconic, used by scholars, craftsmen and students the world over. Automobile engineer, George Carwardine, designed this classic in 1933, using hinges that mimicked the joint of a human arm – and what a clever, novel idea it turned out to be. The Anglepoise is flexible and balanced and can be held in any position you require. Now available in new variations including colours such as primrose yellow, aqua and bubble-gum pink, as well as the more traditional chrome, black, white or silver. There is also a gigantic floor-lamp version for those who want to play Alice in Wonderland.

TIZIO

Where? Aram • 110 Drury Lane, London, WC2 • 00 44 207 557 7557 • www.aram.co.uk
How much? £195/$343/€287
Designed in 1972, Richard Sapper's minimal, energy-efficient aluminium lamp hides the transformer in the base. This reduces voltage, which is conducted through its metal arms to power the lamp, and cleverly eliminates the need for internal wiring. With perfectly counterbalanced arms, this simple but stylish lamp is available in black, white or grey.

LAMP A703

Where? Skandium • 86 Marylebone High Street, London, W1 • 00 44 207 935 2077 • www.skandium.com
How much? £457/$673/€803
Designed by the legendary Finnish designer, Alvar Aalto, with its curved, chrome stand and bubble-shade, this elegant little lamp is chic and unobtrusive. Available in black and white painted metal.

AND A FUN ALTERNATIVE – THE SNOOPY LAMP

Where? TwentyTwentyOne, 274 Upper Street, London, N1 • 00 44 207 288 1996 • www.twentytwentyone.com
How much? £405/$710/€597
So named because it resembles a certain canine cartoon character, this lamp is bursting with personality and humour. More than simply something to illuminate the desk, the Snoopy has all the appeal of a little friend.

Anglepoise desk lamp

Fridge

FAB 28 Smeg Refrigerator

Where?
www.smeguk.com
How much?
Approximately £940/$1,600/€1,378

Who would have thought that the retro-referencing Smeg fridge hasn't actually been around since the fifties, but was instead introduced to the world in 1997? It became an instant design classic, and quite rightly so, its bright colours and curved body making it immediately recognizable.

For domestic divas, labels in the kitchen are as important as they are for other women in the wardrobe. Smeg, therefore, is perfect: free-standing and retro, something that is very 'now' in kitchen design, and the absolute antithesis of the 1990s, when everything had to be hidden.

Smeg stands for 'Smalterie Metallurgiche Emiliane Guastalla', literally 'Metal enamelling factory based in the Reggio Emilia region of Italy', where its factories are still housed today. The company started in the late 1940s by enamelling metal products for the white goods industry. The idea for the FAB fridge came when the Smeg team noted a general yearning towards more ergonomic shapes in domestic design. They copied the distinctive rounded edges of the 1950s' American fridge, adding an enamel exterior in suitably retro shades – cream, pastel blue and pink, for instance – creating an immediate hit.

The FAB is now available in 11 colours, including a Union Jack design. Something you won't want to cover with shopping lists and magnetic poetry.

FAB 28 Smeg Refrigerator

SUB-ZERO

Where? www.subzero.com
How much? Prices from £4,800/$8,425/€7,126
Another brand that gets kitchen obsessives hot under the collar, this label is the polar opposite of Smeg: think sleek lines and a 100 per cent stainless-steel body. For maximum snob appeal, choose one with a glass front, dedicated wine rack and ice-making facilities.

NORCOOL

Where? www.norcool.co.uk
How much? From £2,000/$3,500/€2,900
This is the closest most of us will come to an old-fashioned walk-in larder – a 'fridge pantry' with marble shelves. The Norcool has accurately, if somewhat snidely, been described as suiting the 'middle-class Volvo/Tuscany/farmers-market type who dreams of laying out his unpasteurized cheese and handmade butter on marble'.

Glass / Crystal

Venini & Co

Where?

San Marco, 314 Piazzetta
Leoncini, Venice, Italy •
00 39 041 522 4045 •
www.venini.com

How much?

From £100/$180/€150

In 1921, a Milanese lawyer named Paolo Venini founded a glassware factory in Murano with Giacomo Cappellini, a Venetian antiques dealer, and Vittorio Zecchin, an art director. The simple, impactful designs instantly marked out the brand from its competitors, and a canny move to commission high-profile artists, including Salvador Dali, Carlo Scarpa and Fulvio Bianconi, further added to the company's appeal in the 1930s. Venini's vintage, brightly coloured designs of the 1950s are highly desirable today, with vases fetching up to $10,000 at auction. The company's eternally elegant and highly collectable designs include the 707 glass vase, beautiful champagne flutes and wave-edged bowls.

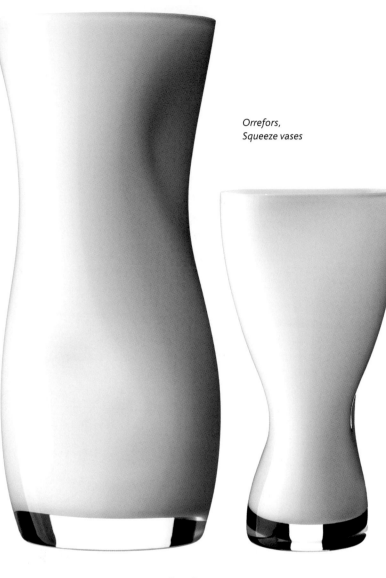

*Orrefors,
Squeeze vases*

ORREFORS

Where? www.orrefors.com • Skandium,
86 Marylebone High Street, London, W1 • 00 44 207 935 2077 • www.skandium.com
How much? From £62.50/$110/€92
This highly respected Swedish company employed artists Simon Gate, Edvard Hald and Vicke Lindstrand to work on its ornamental glass production in the 1930s. Contemporary designs include the delightful 'Squeeze' vase by Lena Bergstrom.

WATERFORD

Where? 173–74 Piccadilly, London, W1 • 00 44 207 629 2614 • www.waterford.co.uk
How much? Metra vase: £180/$316/€265
This British brand was established in 1783, when George and William Penrose founded their business in the port of

Other great glassmakers

Iittala, Finland

This Finnish company sells contemporary glassware – functional but highly stylized.
www.iittala.com

Locchi

A Florentine company that specializes in beautiful cut-glass decanters and glasses.
www.locchi.com

Lalique

Master goldsmith, René Lalique, led the Art Nouveau jewellery movement in the 1890s and later became a top glassmaker; creations include the now iconic bulbous glass rings.
www.lalique.com

LSA International

A 25 year-old British company specializing in contemporary, elegant glassware and particularly good for stylish giant vases. Sturdy but striking glass tableware and very affordable.
www.lsa-international.com

Pasabahçe Beykoz

Turkey's handmade glassware industry is now among the world's most innovative. Come here for marvellous Ottoman-inspired glass tableware.
Tesvikiye Caddesi, 177

Steuben

This US company, founded by the British Frederick Carder, in 1903, takes its name from Steuben Island, where its design studio is located. It is known for its elegant and beautiful vases and bowls.
www.steuben.com

London Antique Glass Directory

Jeanette Hayhurst Fine Glass

A glass gallery specializing in fine specimens from the 17th to the 20th centuries.
32a Kensington Church Street, London, W8
00 44 207 938 1539

Mark J. West

This established shop houses an impressive selection of glass decanters and exquisite wine glasses.
39b High Street, London, SW19
00 44 208 946 2811
www.markwest-glass.com

Liberty

The famed department store sells a wide selection of antique glass perfume bottles, which make brilliant gifts and should brighten any dressing table.
Regent Street, London, W1
00 44 207 734 1234
www.liberty.co.uk

Waterford in Ireland and started producing high-end glassware. The company has stylishly stepped into the modern age with contemporary ranges by Jasper Conran and John Rocha. The beautifully angular Metra vase sums up the brand's elegant aesthetic.

Waterford glasses

Juicer

Champion 2000+

Where?

www.championjuicer.com • www.ukjuicers.com

How much?

Approximately £249/$438/€361

This is a juicer with a cult following thanks to its hippie roots. Champion juicers have been going since 1955, and are still made by the same family firm, based in California, a juice-friendly state if ever there was one. The 2000+ weighs a tonne, takes up too much space in the kitchen and is far from pretty, but that's not the point – it has been scientifically proven that juice from the Champion retains more nutrients from the original fruit or vegetables than any other model on the market. Which, quite frankly, is any juice-a-holic's dream. This nutrient-containing ability is due to the masticating action of the cutter – a rotating stainless-steel blade that can reach nutrients, even those locked away in the skin.

Champion 2000+ Juicer

The Champion is especially skilled with hard fruit and vegetables, is a doddle to clean, and easy to use – you simply feed through the fruit or vegetable and the pulp comes out of the other end looking rather like a 'sausage'. Despite the scores of new juicers on the market today, this is the model still cited as the best by many raw food experts.

MAGIMIX LE DUO

Where? Selected outlets, including: www.amazon.co.uk

How much? £114/$200/€166

With a centrifugal system, meaning the juicer spins the juice from the pulp, this is quiet to use – a blessing in the morning if others in the house are still sleeping – looks good and comes in a range of colours. With juice bars springing up all over the shop – charging upwards of £2.50 ($4.50) a pop – the reasonably priced Le Duo makes financial sense. It even comes with a recipe book.

WARING JUICE EXTRACTOR

Where? Selected outlets, including: www.amazon.com

How much? £170/$300/€248

Another American brand that has been going since the 1960s, this one is easy to operate, and again, of industrial quality. It is also good with hard fruit and vegetables.

Knives

Global

Where?
Various cookware specialists and department stores, including: www.johnlewis.co.uk

How much?
From £215/$378/€312 for a six-knife block

Very sharp, very chic and very expensive, Global knives are made in Japan – a country with a history of producing sharp products, think of the samurai and their swords – and are on every kitchen snob's wish list.

The reason they're so sharp is because the blade is sharpened to a point, instead of bevelled like other knives. Another idiosyncrasy lies in the handle: received wisdom decrees that a good knife should have a 'full tang' – in other words, a blade that goes through to the handle in one piece. Global knives, however, consist of three pieces – the blade and two dimpled metal pieces that make up the handle; all welded together to create a knife that's surprisingly light. A carefully measured amount of sand inside the hollow handle provides perfect balance for the user.

Given Global's worldwide prestige, the company is relatively young – started by Komin Yamada in 1985. All knives are still made in Japan. The six-knife block is everything the amateur cook could ask for, and looks less industrial than the usual Global magnetic block.

With regular sharpening and due care – wash and dry immediately after use and never in a dishwasher – a Global knife will last a lifetime.

Global Knives

HENCKELS
Where? www.zwilling.com • www.theknifeshop.co.uk
How much? From about £35/$62/€51 per knife.
Global's closest competitors are both German companies: Wusthof-Trident and Henckels. The latter is better known and has been making knives since 1731.

LAGUIOLE
Where? www.laguiole-france.com
How much? From about £23/$41/€34 per knife
These knives, first made in 1829 in the French province of the same name, were initially used by shepherds. Today Laguiole make the best steak knives. Especially attractive is the box of six, with each handle crafted from a different type of wood, something that would make any table setting instantly eye-catching.

Oven

Aga

Where?
www.aga-rayburn.co.uk
How much?
£7,100/$12,462/€10,540

Aga Oven

Ovens can make people ridiculously territorial – the chef Gordon Ramsay, for instance, once threatened to lock his domestic model away from his wife. They can also sell houses, especially if they're an Aga, an oven that's become a byword for rural middle-class England.

Agas are special. They use radiant heat so the oven is always ready to cook; the result is that the food is moister than usual, with the flavour sealed in. An Aga's temperatures aren't readily adjustable, as they are on conventional ovens; instead, cooks must rely on intuition, yet once the Aga owner understands his or her cooker's subtleties, anything is possible. Or so the theory goes. Dedicated recipe books for Aga users instruct on where certain foods can be cooked and for how long – a poppadom can be ready in seconds, for instance, by trapping it under the lid of the boiling plate.

Despite being synonymous with all things British, the Aga was actually invented in Sweden in 1922 by Dr Gustav Dalen. The aim of the Nobel Prize-winning Dr Dalen – who was blind, thus never able to see his subsequent design classic – was to create a modern cooker for his wife. Soon after his invention, Agas were manufactured in Britain, a country that immediately took to the cooker's infinite possibilities, as well as its homely style.

A four-oven Aga is the most covetable – this means you can do baking and roasting separately, as well as keeping plates hot in the 'warming oven' – and is available in a range of jolly colours; Aga snobs prefer cream. Ovens come with a wire-folding toaster that can toast four slices at a time when placed on the hotplate – obsessives insist that this makes the perfect slice of toast. Agas can also be used for ironing, to open jam jars and dry out boots … no wonder some cooks go ga-ga for Agas.

VIKING RANGE COOKER
Where? www.vikingrange.com
How much? From approximately £2,825/$5,000/€4,140
The Viking doesn't have a restaurant pedigree – which is a good thing. This is a professional quality cooker designed for home cooks with the same snob-factor appeal for Americans that the Aga has for Brits. Like an Aga, a Viking range can be bought with dual ovens and comes in a range of finishes, including forest green and cobalt blue. Expect kitchen envy with one of these.

LACANCHE CLUNY STEEL RANGE
Where? Various dealers, including: www.appliances.co.uk and www.biasco.com
How much? From approximately £2,500/$4,424/€3,664
'The couture gown of ovens,' according to *Vogue* magazine, the Lacanche Cluny is seriously smart, with five hobs of various sizes, two ovens and storage drawers. Found in stylish urban kitchens.

Paint

Farrow & Ball New White

Farrow & Ball New White

Where?

www.farrow-ball.com

How much?

£21.99/$39/€33 for 2.5 litres (0.7 gallons)

This is the new magnolia: a creamy white that is warmer than most and ideal either on its own or to complement other colours. If glossy brilliant white looks too bright, then New White is more mellow, never looking too modern nor too stark.

Part of New White's appeal is down to its pigment that includes raw umber (a natural brown clay), yellow ochre and a touch of burnt umber to give the shade warmth. The end product has a soft, almost powdery finish, something that is a trademark of posh paint-makers Farrow & Ball.

Another trademark is the company's crazy colour names: Eating Room Red (a deep, aristocratic shade), for instance, or Elephant's Breath (a soft grey). Yet it is their palette of whites for which the company is most renowned – All White, Old White, Strong White and White Tie to name but a few – and choosing exactly which one to use has driven many an amateur decorator mad. New White is the brand's bestseller, created when Off White (another popular shade and the whitest white the National Trust dared to use on the restoration of its properties), looked too grey next to regular white.

Farrow & Ball was founded in 1947, but the company really came to prominence when two old school friends, Martin Ephson and Tom Helme, bought the company in 1992. The duo revamped the brand while staying true to its roots, and still manufacture all the paint they sell using traditional methods. They also use lots of pigment – up to 30 per cent more than other manufacturers – resulting in a greater depth and luminance of colour.

Today Farrow & Ball is a byword for smart interior taste, the brand chosen to paint the whole of Highgrove, the Prince of Wales's estate, and mentioned in many an estate agent's details.

FIRED EARTH

Where? www.firedearth.co.uk

How much? From £22.50/$41/€33 for 2.5 litres (0.7 gallons)

A company best known for its tiles, Fired Earth also does a fantastic range of paints that are perfectly suited to Northern European light. Handily for paint virgins, the palette-like brochure is designed in such a way that colours align to match each other perfectly.

THE PAINT LIBRARY

Where? www.paintlibrary.co.uk

How much? From £23.99/$44/€35 for 2.5 litres (0.7 gallons)

This excellent company will tell you which shades work best in which room, using pointers such as the amount of natural light and the colour of the flooring. Tarlatan, a masculine grey shade, is one of the company's most popular colours.

Piano

Yamaha baby grand

Where?
www.yamaha.co.uk • www.pianoplus.co.uk
How much?
Approximately £7,499/$13,174/€10,957

'No home is complete without a piano.' So said Elton John to David Beckham when giving advice on which piano he should buy as a present for his wife. Posh received a black Yamaha baby grand – Elton's favourite; he also plays on a Yamaha concert grand – with 'For My Darling Victoria' written in gold leaf under the lid.

A Yamaha baby grand is half the size of a concert grand piano. It fits into a smaller space than most baby grands, as it has been designed for the modern house – only a mansion could comfortably cope with a full-sized grand piano. Yet the smaller size doesn't mean a compromise on sound. Grand pianos in general produce a better, more full-bodied sound because their strings are longer. An open lid on a grand improves the sound further letting it flood the room.

Yamaha baby grand

Variations in sound are also linked to where the instrument was made. Yamaha pianos are said to sound fresher and crisper than the lusher, more romantic tones of those produced in Europe or the United States. Jazz musicians therefore prefer the former – both Jools Holland and the jazz legend, John Dankworth, play on Yamaha baby grands – while classical musicians plump for the latter.

YAMAHA U1
Where? www.yamaha.co.uk •
www.soundsmusical.com •
www.beethovenpianos.com
How much? Approximately £5,499/$9,662/€8,036
If space really is an issue, then only an upright piano will do. This is regarded as one of the best – a full upright with longer strings than most, producing more of a grand-like sound.

STEINWAY MODEL B
Where? www.steinway.com
How much? Depending on age, material and condition, anything upwards of £10,000/$17,600/€14,600
For the snob-factor, Steinway & Sons is the ultimate brand, not to say the most expensive. Found in concert halls across the world, along with Bosendorfers and Bechsteins, Steinways are crafted using the finest materials and consist of 12,000 parts that are all made by hand – owners believe this gives each Steinway a unique soul. They are even an investment, worth more the older they become. The seven-foot Model B is most popular.

Quilt

Traditional Amish quilt

Where?

The Old Country Store, 3510 Old Philadelphia Pike,
Intercourse, PA 17534 • www.theoldcountrystore.com

How much?

Prices start at £456/$800/€677

Traditional Amish quilt

The best place to find some *Little House on the Prairie*-style chic is Lancaster County in Pennsylvania, home to America's oldest Amish community and arguably the best quilters in the world.

Quilts are now the third-biggest source of income for most Amish communities, and the quilts of Lancaster County are regarded as having the finest needlework and most unusual colour combinations, often set against a darker background. Look closely, though, and you can see that the stitching isn't always super-smooth – according to lore, Amish quilt-makers deliberately mis-stitch now and then, as they believe only God can be perfect.

For the widest variety of quilts, head to The Old Country Store, housed in a Victorian-era general shop. Here you'll find hundreds of quilts, all locally made using skills that have been passed on from mother to daughter. The best quilts come from a single quilter – one pair of hands means a uniformity of stitching – and some can take up to 800 hours to make, hence the high prices. A percentage of each sale goes to the quilter.

Vintage quilts are the most covetable. In 1960s America there was a quilt revival – a natural result of the homespun hippie movement – something that has continued to this day. Nowadays, many quilts have moved from the bed to the wall, becoming bona fide museum pieces in the process, and are sometimes worth several hundred thousand dollars.

HALF-KILO INDIAN QUILT

Where? Maharani Art, Tambako Market, Jodhpur, India

How much? From approx £40/$70/€58

Some of the best heavy Indian quilts come from Jodhpur and one reputable outlet is Maharani Art, a fabric store in the tangled back streets of the old city. Prices are notably higher than your average Indian market stall, but the quality is higher too – fashion houses such as Hermès, Stella McCartney and Etro buy fabric from the same distributor, and you can rest in the knowledge that, because it's a cooperative, the quilters are getting a decent wage.

CABBAGES & ROSES EIDERDOWN

Where? Cabbages & Roses, 3 Langton Street, London, SW10 • 00 44 207 352 7333 • www.cabbagesandroses.com

How much? Prices from £290/$509/€431 for a single

England's answer to the quilt, the eiderdown is essentially a duvet without a removable cover, so a pleasing design is a must. Cabbages & Roses, the original purveyors of shabby chic, have a fantastic selection of antique eiderdowns in store throughout the year.

Rug

Kashgai weavers

Where?

The market in Isfahan, Iran •
Liberty, Regent Street, London,
W1 • 00 44 207 734 1234 •
www.liberty.co.uk
Fired Earth • www.firedearth.co.uk
Rugs UK • www.rugsuk.com

How much?

From £329/$577/€488

Rugs from Persia – modern-day Iran – are still considered the best in the world. A dedicated rug-hunter should head to the ancient city of Isfahan, once a stop-off point for caravans travelling along the Silk Road, where thousands of rugs can still be found in dusty piles at the market. The most prized are antique or 'semi-antique', a term that refers to a rug that is approximately 40 to 70 years old, and dealers prefer to be paid in dollars. Since many here are sold to wholesalers and shipped abroad, a holiday to Iran isn't absolutely necessary.

Western rug specialists, such as Liberty and Fired Earth, sell a wide range of Iranian rugs. Some of the best come from the Kashgai, a nomadic tribe based in southern Iran. The Kashgai have a strong tradition of weaving. Their rugs are hand-knotted using only the wool from the shoulders and neck of the sheep; the result is a rug that is both fine and firm. The rugs are spun by the women of the tribe and no children are involved in production, an unusual guarantee in the carpet trade. The colours are made using vegetable dyes from materials readily available to the tribe – for instance, the rich red that forms the basis of many rugs comes from the madder root. As for the patterns, most are dominated by an arrangement of rhombs and other motifs including stylized flowers, leaves, birds and animals. And it goes without saying that each piece is unique.

One of the reasons Iranian rugs are so good is that they are used by the same people who weave them – and they desire a quality product just as much as you do. Many sold have been used by the tribe for up to 40 years, but will still be in tip-top condition, since they will only have been walked upon in stockinged feet. However, it is always worth checking that any wear is even and that the fringing is in a good condition.

Incidentally, this is a good time to buy *any* oriental rug, especially antique examples, as they are somewhat unfashionable at the moment. Even those sold in auction houses – many of which are made of silk and include gold and silver threads in their designs – offer good value for money and will go for around half of what they would have cost at the height of the rug boom in the 1980s.

STEPEVI

Where? Stepevi, 274 Kings Road, London, SW3 •
00 44 207 376 7574

How Much? From £450/$796/€656

Turkish rugs may be on a par with Persian, yet a tasteful
modern example is still hard to find. Luckily Stepevi, an
Istanbul-based company, sells some of the best, not to say the
boldest. Colourways change twice yearly; alternatively, create
your own with a bespoke version, finished in just four weeks.

BERBER MARITAL RUG

Where? Bazar Dakhla, 63 Souk Teinturiers, Marrakech, Morocco
How much? From £30/$53/€44

Moroccan rugs and carpets aren't as fine, rare or indeed
expensive as those from Turkey or the Middle East, but they're
still better – and cheaper – than anything you'll find back
home. In Marrakech, head for Bazar Dakhla in the carpet souk
for a wide selection of carpets and rugs, including kilims from
both the High and Middle Atlas Mountains. A good buy is a
Berber marital rug with inlaid mirrors.

Stepevi

*' I go to Morocco two or three times a year for inspiration. One of the best buys is rugs and carpets. I have a hoard
of cream sequinned carpets – originally used as wedding blankets – that cost about £40, and I've seen them in
Liberty for £250. I also invested in a proper carpet last year, a 1960s Beni Ourane. All are unique with distinctive
black and white designs – in fact, World of Interiors did a piece on them recently – and although not cheap (from
about £450) they're a lot less than buying them in Britain. I've seen them in London for £1,000 upwards!'*

Olivia Morris, London-based shoe designer

HOW TO HAGGLE

For many in Africa and Asia, bartering is a national sport.
And, like any sport, there is a stringent set of rules. First,
patience is crucial. The correct bartering etiquette requires
time – something most merchants have in spades – as it
is considered respectful to think carefully when parting
with something as important as money.

Once you show even the slightest iota of interest, the
game begins. Ask the price, and in a merchant's eyes
you've already bought it. Sellers will start at double, triple,
even ten times the amount they'd expect you to pay. Your
first response should be a method-actor-worthy look of
horror that is followed by a bid somewhere below half the
asking price. Mentally decide on the top price you'll pay
and stick with it. Once you reach it, keep repeating it

over and over – the merchant will eventually get the point.
And once you've both decided on a price, it is extremely
rude to back out.

When dealing with antiques, ask the price first before
enquiring about its provenance – that way, you'll sound
like a seasoned buyer. You can also use articles you've
brought from home – pens, T-shirts, etc. – as part of the
deal, especially if the seller has expressed an interest.

It is also worth knowing that most merchants have their
own pecking order of perceived wealth. The Japanese are
charged the highest prices, then the Americans, followed by
Europeans. If you're after a genuine bargain, pretend you're
from some obscure country. And don't feel bad – merchants
are canny and would never part with anything without
turning a profit.

Sofa

Jasper Morrison Cappelini Elan

Where?
SCP Ltd • 00 44 20 7739 1869 • www.scp.co.uk

How much?
From £2946/$5,302/€4,124

If a chair is the most functional item of furniture in the house, then a sofa is the most leisurely. An object designed for relaxing, reclining and lounging, it is the piece of furniture that signifies time off. So which is the best style? There are thousands of different designs to choose from, from the traditional Chesterfields to the minimal Scandinavian models, but none with quite the same style and grace as the Jasper Morrison Cappelini Elan. Minimal and angular, the beautifully simple Elan sofa epitomizes Morrison's quiet, timeless aesthetic and would look equally good in a Georgian town house as it would in a modern loft apartment.

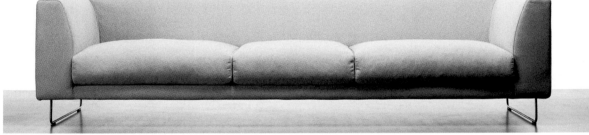

Jasper Morrison Cappelini Elan sofa

ANTONIO CITTERIO CHARLES

Where? B&B Italia, Via Durini 14, 20122, Milan, Italy • 00 39 02 76 44 41
250 Brompton Road, SW3 • 00 44 207 591 8111 • www.bebitalia.co.uk
How much? From £5,000/$8,895/€7,295
The ultimate modular sofa – rectangular, free cushions are placed against a low backrest that make it appear chic and modern. It is also possible to arrange peninsula-shaped compositions in the centre of the room.

Antonio Citterio Charles sofa

FLORENCE KNOLL, MODEL NO. 1205
Where? www.retromodern.com
How much? £2,854/$5,032/€4,184

This clean-lined and elegant sofa was designed in 1954 as part of Florence Knoll's quest to create the ideal 'fill-in pieces'. The solid-wood frame and square tubular steel with a polished chrome finish give it superior stability and style.

*Bocca Marilyn
lips sofa*

Other sofa suppliers

Donghia
Angelo Donghia's furniture company displays American design at its very best. Here you'll find exuberant, impeccably made sofas that fuse classic shapes and modern styling details, for example the beautiful Borsalino collection, which was inspired by the Caribbean style of the 1930s and 1940s.
www.donghia.com

Mascheroni
This luxury Italian brand specializes in large, sleek leather sofas, which fuse traditional manufacturing methods with cool contemporary design. The ethos behind this brand is passion, quality and craftsmanship.
www.mascheroni.it

ILVA
The Danish brand, soon to launch in the UK, create neutral, modern sofas with simple graphic shapes that are both stylish and affordable. Its recent best-selling Toscana sofa – clean lines, cream and utterly chic – is typical of the company's aesthetic. Think of it as the newer, more sophisticated Ikea.
www.ilva.dk

Three iconic sofas

Studio 65, Bocca Marilyn lips sofa You can't get a more inviting couch than one in the shape of a luscious pair of red lips. Inspired by Salvador Dali's Mae West sofa, made in 1936.
www.edra.com

George Nelson's Marshmallow sofa, 1956
This classic has a painted tubular steel frame with vinyl-covered latex foam-filled cushions. Currently available in London at TwentyTwentyOne.
www.twentytwentyone.com

Marcel Breuer couch, 1930–1931
Chromed tubular and flat steel frame with a leather upholstered seat and back cushions, this design classic has been reissued by Tecta.
www.tecta.de

Stationery

Smythson

Where?
40 New Bond Street, London,
W1 • 00 44 207 629 8558 •
www.smythson.com

How much?
Bespoke from £125.50/$225/€175
for 100 cards and envelopes

Smythson stationery

Stationery is having a bit of a moment. Maybe it's a reaction to the prevalence of emails, maybe a yearning back to schooldays when there was always a competition to have the best paper and pens in class. Whatever the reason, when it comes to stationery tread carefully, as the style you choose is very much a statement of how you wish the world to see you. It's all about image, about getting the right size, weight, colour and font. There are stationery snobs out there who will actually turn over letters to check the watermark. So beware.

Smythson stationery will earn you kudos. They are the Queen's favourite stationers with the maximum four royal warrants and have been used in the past by everyone from Sigmund Freud to Grace Kelly. Modern clients include Gwyneth Paltrow, who, as well as using the bespoke service, bought 20 boxes of apple-motif cards when her daughter, Apple, was born. Madonna and her daughter, Lourdes, also have their own individualized sets – the pop icon is very hot on her offspring sending 'thank you' notes, apparently.

The company was founded in 1887 when Frank Smythson started producing lightweight diaries – Princes Harry and William won't use anything else. Stationery quickly followed, as did a bespoke service, which nowadays includes hand-engraved motifs (there are over 100 to choose from, ranging from a ladybird to a black stiletto); tissue-lined envelopes in a variety of colours, hand-painted borders and different typestyles. The lettering is all hand-engraved, which means the lines are just so and the ink is of a perfect intensity.

And the colour? Favourites include Park Avenue Pink, Bond Street Blue and, of course, Nile Blue, the brand's signature shade, found on all its packaging and inspired by a trip Frank once took to Egypt.

CRANE & CO.
Where? www.crane.com • Alastair Lockhart, 97 Walton Street, London, SW3 • 00 44 207 581 8289
How much? From £13.50/$24/€20
The US equivalent of Smythson, Crane & Co. is where the White House gets its stationery and is also the supplier of paper for the US dollar bill. Shoppers should bear in mind that American paper comes in different sizes to British – it is both smaller and squarer.

R. NICHOLS
Where? www.r-nichols.com
How much? From £5.50/$10/€8
Distinctive, fashion-led designs – a typical motif is a woman rushing for a New York taxi laden down with shopping bags. R. Nichols is Manhattan based, perfect for Carrie Bradshaw acolytes everywhere.

Table linen

Busatti Melograno

Where?

14 Via Mazzini, Anghiari, Toscana, Italy, plus branches • 00 39 0575 788 013 • www.busatti.com

How much?

Prices start at £5.40/$9.50/€8

Busatti Melograno

Every host or hostess needs to know how to dress a table beautifully. And like most things, good table dressing starts with a good foundation.

Some of the most beautiful table linens can be found at Busatti. The store is an experience in itself; situated inside the pretty Tuscan walled town of Anghiari, Busatti's showrooms are housed in a vaulted 16th-century building. The family-run company was founded in 1842 and still uses the same 19th-century techniques and antique looms. All the dyes are vegetable-based and the hems are stitched by hand. The result is of a much higher quality than most of us are used to today – the fabric is soft yet washable, *very* necessary for table linen and indeed these tablecloths are investment pieces that will last a lifetime.

Busatti's clientele include Miuccia Prada and Valentino, both fans of the company's custom-made service. Off-the-peg designs have an aristocratic feel – think plenty of jacquards in rich hues – perfect if you hanker after the stately home effect. The Melograno range (pictured above) feels more modern. Its fresh stripes are available in a number of colourways and the fabric is a mix of linen and cotton. Busatti also makes bed linens, which are again wonderfully soft, and upholstery materials.

GIVERNY

Where? www.divertimenti.co.uk

How much? £59.95/$106/€87

This classic red-and-white checked pattern is perfect for anyone aiming for the shabby-chic bistro effect. Just add Duralex tumblers full of red wine and a dripping candle.

DESIGNER'S GUILD

Where? 267 and 277 Kings Road, London, SW3 and branches • 00 44 207 351 5775 • www.designersguild.com

How much? From £8/$14/€12 for a set of 4 placemats

Add a splash of colour to a table of white porcelain plates with a bold print from Designer's Guild. Their signature rangy florals in citrus shades should perk up even the dullest of dinner parties.

Teapot

Mariage Frères

Where?
30 Rue du Bourg-Tibourg,
75004, Paris, France •
00 33 1 42 72 28 11 •
www.mariagefreres.com

How much?
£81/$144/€120

Loukoum teapots

The French are in the throws of a love affair with tea, hanging out in tea salons and treating different blends with the kind of reverence they would normally reserve for fine wine or good coffee.

So it makes sense that Paris has also become the premiere teapot-purchasing destination in the world. Mariage Frères is the city's most celebrated salon – Hugh Grant is one of many celebrity fans of this curiously olde-worlde establishment in the heart of the Marais district, and the actress Isabelle Adjani takes tea here every week.

There is a museum on the second floor, up a very creaky staircase, but the main pull is the shop itself – a veritable tea heaven, crammed with hundreds of varieties of world-class blends, including more than 50 types of Darjeeling. The teas are displayed in row upon row of canisters, ready to be dispensed into pretty little tins, the pride of any kitchen.

Also displayed in the shop's wooden cabinets are teapots, some cast iron, some porcelain, but all extremely stylish. Their Loukoum design is one of the best, a pleasing combination of Oriental wit with Western overtones in a range of striking colours: think turquoise, orange and coral. A matching Japanese-style handle-free cup is also available.

Nicolas Mariage was one of the first merchants to introduce tea to France, yet his teas have only been on sale to the general public since the 1980s; before that, only a select few, including Russia's last tsar, Nicholas II, were deemed sufficiently worthy of supping the brews. Nowadays, Mariage Frères is open to all and, since tea parties are the new cocktail parties, there's no excuse to lay a less-than-chic table.

TAKASHIMAYA
Where? 693 Fifth Avenue, between 54th and 55th Streets, New York, 10022, NY • 00 1 212 350 0100 • www.ny-takashimaya.com
How much? From £26/$45/€38
The Manhattan outpost of this Japanese department store sells only the most design-conscious oriental objects. Takashimaya's weighty cast-iron teapots are part of the traditional – and very ritualized – way the Japanese take tea. To get an idea of the experience, visit the Tea Box, Takashimaya's in-store café where the sushi is cut to look like finger sandwiches. *Kawaiiiii!* (cute!), as the Japanese might say.

ROYAL ALBERT OLD COUNTRY ROSES
Where? www.royaldoulton.com
How much? £76/$137/€112 for a large teapot
You can't talk teapots without mentioning this one, officially the world's best-selling design. A chintz-tastic pattern – and, quite frankly, as English as it gets.

Tiles

Hand-painted Portuguese azulejos

Where?

Sant'Anna Tile Factory, 96 Calcada da Boa Hora, Lisbon, Portugal • 00 351 21 363 8292

Sant'Anna Showroom, 95 Rua do Alecrim, Lisbon • 00 351 21 342 2537.

How much?

From around £4.50/$8/€7 for a tile

Portuguese tiles

Whiz around the streets of Lisbon and you'll quickly realize that tiles *(azulejos)* are omnipresent, decorating the exteriors of the most innocuous of buildings and the interiors of everything from barbershops to butchers.

Sant'Anna is regarded as the one of the best tile producers in Europe. The company specializes in historic reproduction tiles, but will also make bespoke pieces. This traditional producer hasn't changed much in the last 200 years and all tiles are still made by hand; the pattern stencilled onto a plain white tile before being painted and then glazed. Helpful showroom staff will make your choice less time-consuming, pulling out heavy panels of completed sets so customers can see the design in its full glory. As well as reproductions, there is a small selection of antique tiles, mostly framed for use as stand-alone decorative pieces. Sant'Anna will also ship your tiles home so there's no need to worry about them weighing down your luggage.

SOCIÉTÉ FAKHKHARI

Where? Avenue Altal Ben Abdallah, Fez, Morocco

How much? From around £2/$3.50/€2.90 per tile

Morocco is another country famed for its tiles, and those from Fez are superior to any found in Marrakech, as Fez clay is rich in manganese and therefore more scratch-proof. Try the workshops in the Quartier de Poterie, or the Société Fakhkhari. Situated just outside the medina, this is a pile-it-high store with the advantage, for anyone suffering from haggle-fatigue, of fixed prices – although this being Morocco, deals can still be done, especially if you pay in cash. Since the factory is next door to the shop, prices are rock bottom and for once the quality is superb. The Societé also produces whole mosaic floors that can be shipped anywhere in the world.

TALAVERA SANTA CATARINA

Where? Santa Catarina Workshop, Cholula, Puebla, 77820, Mexico • 00 52 222 247 6614

How much? From around £5.70/$10/€8.50 for a mural tile

Like Lisbon, Puebla in Mexico is a city covered in tiles. Tin-glazed 'Poblano Talavera' tiles are a speciality, although there are only a few authentic workshops remaining. Talavera Santa Catarina is one of them – here you'll find the real deal in bright cobalt blues, yellows, greens and ochre.

Toaster

Dualit

Where?

Various cookware specialists and department stores, including: www.johnlewis.co.uk • www.amazon.com

How much?

From £109/$192/€158 for a two-slice model

Dualit

A kitchen classic that's spawned scores of imitators, and justly so, as the Dualit toaster does all the right things – it looks good *and* makes great toast.

The British company Dualit has been making toasters for more than 50 years and its models are a favourite with all the top hotels, where a constant supply of hot toast is a must for the daily routine of breakfast. Instead of popping up, the Dualit is manually operated, switching itself off when the toast is ready and keeping it warm until you're set to add butter. The bread slots are wider than most, so they can accommodate waffles and teacakes; add a sandwich cage, and Dualit can also do a cracking toastie. Each toaster is assembled by hand and you can choose from two-, four- or six-slice options in a number of fashionable retro colours, including lavender, duck-egg blue and fire-engine red, as well as chrome.

If that wasn't enough, Dualit even has eco-awareness on its side, as the toasters' ability to do one slice of toast at a time with a single plate means no electricity is wasted.

SIEMENS PORSCHE DESIGN TOASTER

Where? www.siemens.com

How much? £99.95/$176/€145

As the name implies, this slim brushed-steel model is designed by the car manufacturers. With an illuminated browning display – perfect for midnight snack sessions – and 11 levels of toasting, this two-slicer is the ultimate bachelor pad toaster.

KITCHENAID'S PRO LINE TWO-SLICE TOASTER

Where? www.kitchenaid.com • department stores

How Much? £169/$300/€247

Desirability-wise, this brand is up there with the Dualit. As well as a pleasingly retro design, the Pro Line model has extra-wide and thick slots to fit the chunkiest of bagels.

Towels

Hammacher Schlemmer

Where?
147 East 57th Street, between Lexington and Third Avenues. New York, NY 10022 • 00 1 212 421 9000 • www.hammacher.com

How much?
Prices from £17/$29.95/€25

A selection of Turkish towels from Hammacher Schlemmer

What is it about fluffy white towels? Is it their cocooning quality? The super-luxe-factor? Or merely the fact that towels with a deep pile can dry you in next to no time at all – what bliss!

When it comes to quality control, towels are rather like sheets, rated by weight and provenance. Turkish-made are best, closely followed by Egyptian cotton. As for weight, the heavier they are, the deeper the pile, which makes them more effective as well as longer-lasting. Spend more, in other words, and your towels will be an investment in the long run.

Hammacher Schlemmer is a New York institution. Founded in 1848, the store has only ever had one mission: 'To find quality.' The result, thanks to their in-house institute, which researches and tests each of the products they sell, is the best the world has to offer. The towels sold here come from the Denizli region of Turkey, an area known for towelling of extraordinary thickness. They are 800g (28oz) in weight, the densest available, and with a 6mm (¼-inch) pile that means they're very, very soft.

The Manhattan-based designer Michael Kors swears by Hammacher's towels – and you know how fussy fashion folk are. 'I love the minute when my white towels are no longer white, as it means that I can simply replace them with new ones,' he says, and he admits to buying new towels every three weeks for his Fire Island holiday home.

SCENES DE LIN
Where? 70 Rue de la Liberté, Marché du Guéliz, 4000, Marrakech, Morocco • 00 212 444 36108
How much? Prices from £5.55/$9.75/€8.25
This well-edited shop, the perfect escape from the heat, smell and dust of the souk, stocks everything a fabulously designed home could want, including giant hamam-style fringed towels. Hamam towels are generally rougher than most – all the better for a spot of exfoliation. Scenes de Lins' designs also look very stylish.

TERESA ALECRIM
Where? 76 Rua Nova do Almada, Lisbon, Portugal • 00 351 21 342 1831
How much? From £15/$27/€22
Portugal is a brilliant destination for bathroom gear – think fantastic-smelling soaps, cheap colognes and fabulous towels. *Vogue* recommends Teresa Alecrim, a place that has been described as 'Portugal's answer to Laura Ashley', for its embroidered monogrammed towels, a style popular in Lisbon.

Wallpaper

Florence Broadhurst

Where?
Signature Prints
www.signatureprints.com.au •
www.borderlinefabrics.com
How much?
£144/$265/€211 per roll.

A selection of Florence Broadhurst's prints

We've voted Florence Broadhurst number one as her unique prints – bold designs that fuse metallic and tropical shades – have single-handedly spurred the current renaissance in wallpaper, convincing a younger paint-obsessed audience that it needn't be kitsch.

The Japanese Floral print, which features large flowers opened up like a fan, is regarded as her most iconic design, found in New York's branch of Soho House, for instance. It comes in a number of colourways including silver, aubergine, lemon yellow and bright orange. Everything is made to order and all Broadhurst papers are screen-printed by hand. Other classic prints include Imperial Brocade, a new take on classic flock, Tiger Stripes, Horses Stampede and Japanese Bamboo.

Originally from the Australian outback, Broadhurst spent some time living in Asia, where she founded an academy of modern arts, as well as Europe – she had a dress salon in Paris. After describing Australia as a 'desert that likes to buy beige', she established a wallpaper studio. Broadhurst's flamboyant lifestyle made her a minor celebrity, but it was her company that gave her kudos – she continued creating two new designs a week until her death in 1977. 'My success is the fact that my wallpapers have now become a status symbol,' she once commented.

Florence Broadhurst's wallpapers lay forgotten until 1990, when her archive was discovered in a warehouse. The couple behind the discovery started a company – Signature Prints – and began distributing the designs across the globe. Today, the Signature Prints team works non-stop to satisfy demand. Some lucky homeowners in Sydney's more affluent suburbs still have original Broadhurst designs on their walls, while the Butterfly Room in the city's State Theatre sports a Broadhurst paper that now has protected status.

COLE & SON

Where? www.cole-and-son.com
How much? From £80/$147/€117 per roll
Exotic birds always make a popular print, and Hummingbirds from Cole & Son, a manufacturer with a royal warrant, manages to remain traditional, but not in the least bit boring. A classic.

TAPETTITALO

Where? www.tapettitalo.fi
How much? £28/$53/€42
Tapettitalo is a Finnish company that makes some fantastic papers in prints that aren't commonplace – well, not yet. The Skylark design is their signature print, but Cherry Tree, a succession of cherry blossoms, is more subtle.

Jewellery

'It would be very glamorous to be reincarnated as a great big ring on Liz Taylor's finger.'

Andy Warhol, artist, 1928–87

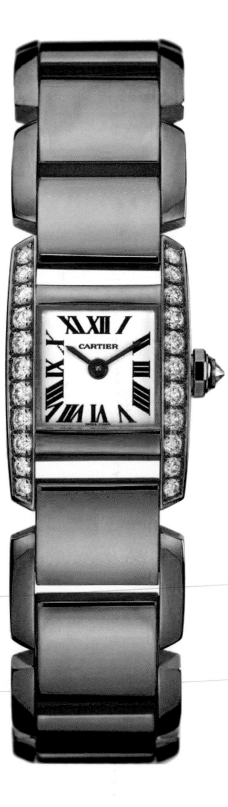

Cufflinks

Longmire Stirrup cufflinks

Where?

10 New Bond St, London, W1 • 00 44 207 930 8720 • www.longmire.co.uk

How much?

From £6,700/$12,206/€9,956

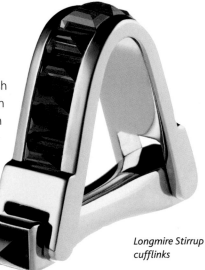

For such a simple, practical accessory, it is still hard to find a truly stylish pair of cufflinks. The world seems full of tacky novelty varieties, which do a man's cuffs and credibility no good. Originating in the 19th century, cufflinks are a relatively new accessory for men and glide between the practical and decorative – they are as useful as a button, but double as a fine piece of jewellery. So, where do you go to find the best cufflinks a man can get? Straight to Longmire, the independent English jeweller that has long been producing fine and unique cufflinks – and holds that all-important royal warrant. Inspired by the Art Deco designs of the 1930s, the stirrup style has cut sapphires mounted in solid 18-carat white gold and wraps around the edge of the cuff. All very stylish indeed. The New Bond Street shop will also make a pair to your precise requirements.

Longmire Stirrup cufflinks

ASPREY 167 BUTTON PAVÉ

Where? 167 New Bond Street, London, W1 • 00 44 207 493 6767 • www.asprey.com

How much? £2,800/$5,106/€4,156

Asprey's 167-button pavé cufflinks are understated, elegant and have just a hint of bling, hailing from the shop that Elizabeth Taylor and Richard Burton frequented in their heyday. But if this style doesn't tickle your fancy, don't worry, as Asprey's fine fleet of silversmiths and jewellers are available to carry out custom-made commissions in workshops above the Bond Street premises.

Asprey 167 button pavé cufflinks

CARTIER

Where? 13, Rue de la Paix, Paris, 75002, France • 00 33 1 44 55 32 50 • www.cartier.com • 40–41 Old Bond Street, London, W1 • 00 44 207 290 5150

How much? From about £1000/$1823/€1484

The classic French jewellery brand specializes in diamonds, so its 18-carat yellow-gold cufflinks encrusted in the classic Cartier initials are utterly desirable.

Diamond ring

Wint & Kidd

Where?

237 Westbourne Grove, London, W11 • The Courtyard, Royal Exchange, London, EC3 •
00 44 207 908 9990 • www.wintandkidd.com

How much?

Price on application

In the 1944 Alfred Hitchcock film *Lifeboat*, the star isn't the gorgeous, pouting Tallulah Bankhead; instead it's a glittering Cartier diamond bracelet. When a Nazi captain discovers the piece – left by Tallulah after her boat is bombed – he ponders: 'They're really nothing but a few pieces of carbon.'

Men, eh? They just don't get diamonds. They don't understand how a little sparkle is good for the soul; how a pair of diamond studs can magically brighten the complexion; how a diamond – a real one, that is, not a manmade rock – is a miracle of nature, each one utterly unique; why diamonds are old-school glamour; and why they really are a girl's best friend.

Thank goodness, then, that diamonds are no longer the preserve of heirloom-fortuitous blue bloods. A combination of clever marketing, accessibility – cheap internet websites, for example www.cooldiamonds.com – and bling hip-hop stars means that the diamond market is now worth £34 ($60) billion a year, the highest it has ever been. This increased popularity has also meant an increase in awareness of the appalling mining conditions suffered by most diamond workers, and certain brands, which shall remain nameless, are targets of placard-heavy protests, a somewhat incongruous sight on the world's glitzier shopping streets.

Wint & Kidd are diamond dealers with a difference. Not only do they possess an almost unrivalled selection of coloured diamonds – only one in 10,000 diamonds mined is coloured – but the company also puts money back into Angola, where they source their stones, to house, feed and educate street children. Wint & Kidd, in other words, is one of the few ethical faces in a trade riddled with human cruelty.

But ethics shouldn't be the only reason you choose Wint & Kidd. Their jewellery settings are discreet, making the most of the stone, something that is surprisingly rare in modern jewellery design, and they also make pieces to order. In addition, their shops, which are designed by Matthew Williamson, don't feel in the least bit mass-market, with helpful and knowledgeable staff on hand.

Their range of coloured diamonds is exquisite. Coloured diamonds are among some of the most valuable objects on Earth, their brilliant hues the result of impurities entering the stones as they form. The most rare are red, closely followed by green, purple, violet, orange, blue, pink and yellow. Wint & Kidd stocks them all – as well, of course, as the more usual white.

Wint & Kidd

HARRY WINSTON

Where? www.harry-winston.com
How much? From £8,500/$15,000/€12,700
Established in 1932, the superstar jeweller is now synonymous with the Academy Awards – many an actress believes his baubles are lucky charms. Perfect if you're looking for household-name kudos combined with clever designs.

DIAMOND LAND

Where? Diamond Land, Appelmansstraat 334, Antwerp 2018, Belgium • 00 32 32 29 29 90 • www.diamondland.be
How much? From about £2,000/$3,500/€2,900 for a one-carat stone
Antwerp has been the world's diamond centre since the 15th century, when the Flemish invented the technique of polishing

Harry Winston ring

stones. Even today, half the world's polished stones – and seven out of ten rough diamonds – change hands here. There are around 1,500 diamond companies, the best of which are along the Pelikaanstraat. Look for a shop with an ADJA (Antwerp Diamond Jewellers Association) sticker in the window. The largest is Diamond Land, a reliable place to start your hunt.

DEALING IN DIAMONDS

The secret to clever diamond shopping is to understand the four Cs – carat, clarity, colour and cut. Carat refers to the size of the diamond and clarity refers to the flawless quality of the stone. As for the cut, there are a number to choose from: pear, round, marquise or princess, for instance; marquise and pear-shaped diamonds are the most flattering on shorter fingers. Uncut diamonds, which resemble pieces of unpolished glass, are also known as 'rough diamonds', and are gaining popularity as a novel way to wear the stone. Really, what could be more decadent?

ROCK STARS

• The biggest diamond ever was the Cullinan, which was found in a South African mine in 1905 and weighed 3,106 carats (0.76kg/1.67lb) uncut. It was presented to King Edward VII as a birthday gift, who chose the Asscher brothers of Amsterdam as the cutters. It was a prestigious, if somewhat daunting, honour – when the initial split was performed, one of the brothers actually fainted from the stress. The Cullinan ended up as 105 stones, the brothers receiving 102 of them as payment. The two biggest, the Great Star and Lesser Star of Africa, became part of the British Crown Jewels. The pear-shaped 550.2-carat Great Star is still the largest polished diamond in the world, forming part of the Royal Sceptre.

• The Koh-i-Noor, a duck-egg shaped diamond that forms part of the British Crown Jewels, is the most famous of all diamonds. It is by no means the biggest diamond in the Tower of London; instead its fame derives from its tumultuous history. According to legend, the 600-carat diamond was discovered on the forehead of an abandoned child of the Hindu sun god on the banks of the Yamuna River. The gem passed from the Mughals to the Afghans to the Sikhs, several of its owners dying to protect it. A 6th-century valuation estimated that it was worth half the daily expenditure of the whole world. Then, in 1849, the British seized the stone and presented it to Queen Victoria. The monarch had a passion for gems – she preferred wearing her own to heirlooms – and ordered it to be cut and set into one of her crowns.

Gems

Gem Palace

Where?

M.I. Road, Jaipur, 302001, India • 00 91 141 2374 175 • www.gempalacejaipur.com

How much?

Price on application

Rajasthan is *the* place for gem shopping and Jaipur its epicentre, in particular the shops along Haldion Ka Rasta and Gopalji da Rasta, near the Hawa Mahal. Here you'll find men cutting and polishing stones in dusty workshops, mostly for a made-to-measure market. For a more ordered environment, head to the Gem Palace and gasp at the bowlfuls of loose gems – rubies, emeralds, diamonds, opals, aquamarines, amethysts, tourmalines and sapphires – displayed as casually as if they were candy.

The Gem Palace is world famous for its bespoke jewellery, and rightly so. Since 1852, the Kasliwal family has traded jewels to Indian royalty and celebrities like Mick Jagger, as well as European jewellery houses such as Bulgari and Cartier. Inside, the store is a veritable jewellery box. As well as loose stones, there are several ready-to-wear lines – the one by acclaimed Parisian jeweller Marie-Hélène de

Loose gems

Taillac is especially recommended and targets Western tastes. But the real joy here is going bespoke. Simple custom-made designs can be completed in a couple of hours. It is the Indian custom to buy stones by weight and then have them strung – the more complex designs are usually worked upon by the Kasliwal brothers themselves. The Gem Palace also sells exquisite antique jewellery.

POPLI

Where? Suleman Chambers, Battery Street, Apollo Bunder, Mumbai, 400039, India • 00 91 22 2202 2321

How much? A ruby necklace starts from £200/$350/€290

Popli in Mumbai has cheap rubies, garnets, sapphires and pearls aplenty, either loose or in strands. Liz Hurley is a regular customer.

FIONA KNAPP

Where? 178a Westbourne Grove, London, W11 • 00 44 207 313 5941 • www.fionaknapp.com
How much? Prices from £800/$1,404/€1,188

This New Zealand-born jeweller is relatively new on the scene, but she has already made a significant impact with bold designs that make the most of brightly hued stones – think pink sapphires and cerise tourmalines. Her pieces are future classics.

Pink gold and pink sapphire Dandelion ring

Oval mosaic aquamarine

Men's rubellite cufflinks

GLOBETROTTING GEM SHOPPING

Savvy shoppers buy their precious stones fresh from the mines, so knowing what comes from where is crucial.

Emeralds

Most come from South America, in particular Columbia. The best mines are in Muzo, Chivor and Cosquez and stones from these sites are a velvety, rich green. Bogota, the country's capital, is fast becoming the world's emerald marketing centre. Brazil, Zimbabwe, Madagascar and the Zambia, where the stones are an unusual bluish-green, are other rich sources.

Rubies

Rubies are the most valuable stone of all, and Mogok in Myanmar (Burma), an area that is known as the Valley of Rubies, is where you'll find the best in the world.

Gems

Museum and Gem Mark on Kaba Aye Pagoda Road, also in Myanmar, are reliable local dealers. Many of these gems end up in Thailand, an important centre for the ruby trade. The most prized shade is known as 'pigeon's blood red', a colour that is deep and rich.

Sapphires

These gems come in a variety of colours, including yellow and pink sapphires. A pink-orange colouring, which is known as a Padparadshah sapphire, is the most prized of all, closely followed by the cornflower-blue sapphires, which are found in Kashmir. Sri Lanka is the best place to go if you're looking for blue sapphires. Australia is currently the world's largest producer of sapphires, but these are not necessarily the prettiest – most are of an inky blue-black hue.

Gold

Garrard

Where?
24 Albermarle St, London, W1 • 00 44 207 758 8520 •
www.garrard.com

How much?
From £1,000/$1,764/€1,467 for a gold band

Garrard

Gold has been used in many different guises, from currency to crowns for teeth. It was first used by prehistoric man, and the oldest gold jewellery – discovered by archaeologists in the Sumerian Royal Tombs at Ur, now in Southern Iraq – is thought to date back to around 3000 BC. At about the same time, the ancient Egyptians were beating gold into leaf, as well as alloying it with other metals. In 1352 BC, the young Egyptian King, Tutankhamen, was interred in a pyramid tomb laden with gold, his remains placed in an extravagant gold anthropoid sarcophagus. When the tomb was opened, it revealed an incredible 1,110kg-(2,448lb-) gold coffin and hundreds of gold and gold-leafed objects.

So what are the origins of the gold wedding band? Dating back to Egyptian times and also used by the Romans, the ring is thought to simply resemble life and eternity. But it wasn't always so glamorous; wedding bands were simply iron hoops until the second century AD, when the true beauty, lustre and resistance of gold was fully realized.

Dating back to 1722, when original founder George Wickes entered Goldsmiths Hall, Garrard is most famous for making royal crowns. Now, with Jade Jagger at the helm, the luxury jeweller has managed to step into the 21st century and is without doubt one of the most glamorous places to go for a classic gold wedding band.

DINH VAN
Where? 15, Rue de la Paix, 75002, Paris, France • 35b Sloane Street, London, SW1 • www.dinhvan.co.uk
How much? From £250/$444/€367 for a wedding band
Vietnamese-born, Paris-raised goldsmith, Jean Dinh Van, worked for Cartier in the 1950s and 1960s and now produces some of the most exquisite and luxurious gold designs in the world. The gold bands are gorgeous.

ME & RO
Where? 241 Elizabeth Street, New York, 10012 • 00 1 917 237 9215 • www.meandrojewelry.com
How much? From £263/$465/€385 for an 18-carat lotus gold pendant
Hip New York-based designers, Michele Quan and Robin Renzi, create pretty modern bracelets, necklaces and earrings with a hint of ethnicity in 18-carat gold.

Gold for less

Istanbul, India and Greece are just a few of the countries where you can find beautifully designed gold on the cheap. In Greece, A. Patrikiadou is notable for selling excellent Byzantine jewellery dating back as far as the 4th century BC. Istanbul is brilliant for buying intricately designed gold at very reasonable prices – it is just a matter of haggling a bit here and there, while Tribhovandas Bhimji Zaveri in Mumbai, India, has five floors of gold and gems to riffle through. (A. Patrikiadou, 58 Pandrossou, Athens, Greece 00 30 210 325 0539; Tribhovandas Bhimji Zaveri, 241-43 Zaveri Bazaar, Mumbai, India 00 91 22 2363 3060.)

Pearls

Mikimoto

Where?

www.mikimoto.com • www.mikimotoamerica.com

How much?

Pictured: 41mm- (16in-) Akoya cultured pearl single strand with 5.5mm-6mm- (⅕in-) pearls and gold clasp £1,730/$3,037/€2,568

Mikimoto

Pearl devotees are as classy as they come: think Coco Chanel and the long strings that decorated her black bouclé suits, Audrey Hepburn in *Breakfast at Tiffany's* and the Queen. Although organic in form, pearls are classed as a precious stone. They are an essential element to any jewellery box and a good set will make an outfit. But what makes a good set?

For a start, the pearl purchaser must know about natural versus cultured pearls. Only about one per cent of all pearls are natural. These true pearls, a beauty born of irritation, are known as 'oriental pearls' and come from molluscs known as pearl oysters, found mainly in the Persian Gulf, Red Sea and the Gulf of Manaar, between India and Sri Lanka. An irritant enters the oyster and is then surrounded with thin layers of nacre, or mother-of-pearl (a protein consisting of calcium) until a pearl has been formed; the thicker the layers of nacre, the more lustrous the pearl.

Mikimoto provides the best cultured-pearl necklaces, primarily because they leave the oysters alone in the nacre-building stage for the longest. Kokichi Mikimoto, the son of a noodle restaurant owner, acquired a patent for the pearl-culturing process in the early 1900s. His ambition was to make enough pearls to 'adorn the neck of every woman in the world'. Since then, the label has farmed Akoya pearl oysters, assisting the conception, letting the oysters grow for two years, and then inserting a mother-of-pearl bead into the shell. The oyster is then left for at least a further two years, during which time the nacre should have built up.

A velvety pink lustre makes a pearl highly prized. Other factors include the size – pearls are measured in grains – and shape; the perfect pearl should have a smooth, unblemished skin. A good quality-control test is to use your teeth – proper pearls should feel gritty when passed against them.

A single strand is the most elegant and versatile; more strands – à la Coco Chanel – are good for the evening. And it's true that regular wear is good for pearls, as they gain lustre from regular contact with the oils found in the skin. There really is no excuse then, so get on your pearls, girls!

TIFFANY & CO.

Where? www.tiffany.com

How much? Prices from £650/$1,141/€965

Recently, this world-famous jeweller has adopted the 'something besides diamonds' approach and introduced a small collection of pearl pieces. Expect fresh, clean, modern designs.

SOUTH SEA PEARLS

Where? Specialized outfits, for example www.pearlparadise.com

How much? Several thousand pounds/dollars/euros per pearl

Along with Tahitian examples, these natural pearls are the best – and the biggest at more than 10mm (⅕in) in diameter. They are found in silver, black and gold.

> '*You can turn an absolute whore into a lady by just putting pearls round her neck.*'
>
> **Donald Brooks, Broadway costume designer**

Silver jewellery

Links of London

Where?

16 Sloane Square, London, SW1 • 00 44 207 730
3133 • www.linksoflondon.com

How much?

From about £150/$273/€223 for a silver bracelet and three
charms

Links of London

Charm bracelets are one of fashion's most curious inventions, simultaneously the ultimate in glamour and the epitome of cute, youthful chic. The allure of the charm bracelet will never fade, it seems, and if you look at its rich and varied history, it's no wonder. Cowrie-shell bracelets date back thousands of years and were originally worn to promote fertility and wealth. But the charm bracelet as we know it became popular in 19th century Europe, no doubt helped by a host of high profile wearers. These included Queen Victoria, who wore a cameo of her husband on a bracelet after his death, Marlene Dietrich, who used charms for luck when flying and Grace Kelly, who wore one in the 1954 film *Rear Window*. Modern-day charm fans include style icons as diverse as Jade Jagger, J-Lo, Sarah Jessica Parker and Kelly Osbourne. The charm bracelet is particularly appealing in silver, the metal that has been used for coins by the caesars, giant urns by the maharajas, and trinkets by the khans – that it is steeped in history only adds to its allure.

Founded in 1990 by Annoushka Ducas and her husband, John Ayton, after a simple request for a pair of fish cufflinks, Links of London has become the leader of the charm bracelet pack. There is even a special in-store charm bar, where you can have your bracelet customized. A Links of London charm is surprisingly affordable, stylish and very cute.

TIFFANY & CO.

Where? www.tiffany.com

How much? From £125/$222/€183

Established in New York in 1837 and famous for adorning Audrey Hepburn in the classic film *Breakfast at Tiffany's*, Tiffany & Co. remains one of the world's most glamorous silversmiths and is known for its sterling silver 'Heart Tag' charm bracelet.

PATRICK MAVROS

Where? 104–106 Fulham Road, London, SW3 • 00 44 207
052 0001 • www.patrickmavros.com

How much? £225/$410/€334

With nine irresistible animal charms, this lovely bracelet, which is fashioned by London's king of silver, Patrick Mavros, is made in a choice of two lengths: 17.5cm (7in) and 19.7cm (8in).

Patrick Mavros

Georg Jensen necklace

Georg Jensen rings

Classic silver

If it's classic silver you are looking for, Mappin & Webb (www.mappin-and-webb.co.uk), one of the UK's most established silversmiths, has an excellent range of high-quality items, from earrings to bracelets and rings. Danish silversmith Georg Jensen (www.georgjensen.com) offers a very desirable selection of contemporary silver homeware, including cutlery and coffee pots, which are fashioned in a typically streamlined Scandinavian style. Tiffany & Co., also famous for its silverwear, offers some classically chic pieces by Elsa Perretti, from iconic heart-shaped pendants to mirror compacts, all of which make excellent gifts.

EXPERT SILVERSMITH AND SILVER SCULPTOR, PATRICK MAVROS, GIVES THE LOW-DOWN ON SILVER SHOPPING:

How is silver different in attitude to gold?
Patrick Mavros: 'Silver is less formal, yet designed and crafted wisely it can be transformed into something more spectacular than the yellow metal. Silver is softer to look at and is often more flattering on a face or wrist than gold.'

Where does the best silver quality originate?
PM: 'Pure silver, otherwise known as fine silver, has the same quality around the world, yet the richest reefs of ore are found in the ancient mines of Central and South America.'

How is it mined?
PM: 'Either as silver-bearing ore or as a by-product of gold mining, in the same way that other metals are mined in the Earth's crust.'

Are there different grades of silver?
PM: 'Fine silver is alloyed with copper to give it strength. The end result is sterling silver. Other alloys are used depending on whether the silver will be used for enamelling or soldering.'

How can you tell if silver is of a superior quality?
PM: 'Silver must have an even, lustrous surface, with no porosity marks – these look like bubbles or stain-like blemishes. Hallmarks, the most visible sign of all, will tell you if silver is sterling or not.'

How do you clean silver?
PM: 'Most pieces of jewellery can be cleaned by rubbing them gently with a silver cleaning-cloth. These cloths are obtainable from most jewellers or stores that have silver departments. Some silver dipping solutions are also excellent cleaners. Just remember to rinse your jewellery afterwards with clean water. Silver foam can also be used.'

Watch for men

Rolex Oyster

Where?
Rolex stores worldwide • www.rolex.com
Watches of Switzerland •
www.watches-of-switzerland.co.uk

How much?
From £2,000/$3,529/€2,933

This legendary Swiss watchmaker was founded by German businessman Hans Wilsdorf in 1905 and remains leader of the pack. Innovations have included the self-winding watch, which was introduced in 1931 and is powered by an internal mechanism that uses the movement of the wearer's arm. James Bond wore a Rolex Submariner (pictured right), but it is the black-faced Oyster Perpetual that is most desirable watch in the world. All 220 of its components are assembled by hand.

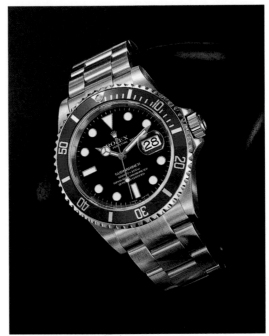

Rolex Oyster Perpetual Submariner

*Breitling
Bentley 6.75*

BREITLING BENTLEY 6.75
Where? www.breitling.com • Watches of Switzerland (as above)
How much? £13,335/$25,527/€19,514
Oozing masculinity, this chunky hunk of a watch resembles the engine of the impressive Bentley Arnage limousine that inspired its design. The Breitling was originally designed for aviation use, as the extra large face provides good visibility.

FRANCK MULLER
Where? www.franckmuller.com • Watches of Switzerland
How much? £39,720/$70,340/€58,464
A relative newcomer to the watch industry, Swiss horologist Franck Muller established his brand in 1990, after learning his trade and finishing top of the class at Geneva's famous Ecole d'Horologerie. His large, angular, diamond-encrusted watch has equal measures of manliness and grace.

A SHORT HISTORY OF TIMEKEEPING

Early measurements of time were initially based on observations of seasonal cycles, while shorter intervals were measured by observing the shadow cast by an upright object, such as a sundial. Then came the hourglass, followed by the 'clepsydra', a water clock that measured the flow of liquid from a container. The earliest watches were ornate and date back to the 1500s, but the first mechanical, machine-made watches were invented as late as the 1850s. The first modern-looking wristwatch evolved in the 1900s, although pocket watches were still popular until the Second World War, when service men found smaller wristwatches more practical. Although the digital watch was invented in the 1960s, it is the classic Swiss-made dial watch that reigns as the most discerning timepiece.

Watch for women

Cartier Tankissme

Where?
Cartier, 40–41 Old Bond St, London, W1 • 00 44 207
290 5150 • www.cartier.com

How much?
£13,925/$24,658/€20,491

Founded in 1847 by Parisian Louis-François Cartier, the company, which is well known for its diamond-studded designs, first opened a London boutique in 1902. The 18-carat, white-gold, diamond-set Tankissme watch is timelessly elegant with a small, square face, diamond edging and chunky white-gold silver links.

HERMÈS CAPE COD
Where? Hermès stores worldwide • www.hermes.com
How much? Around £700/$1,250/€1,000
With its chic double tan strap, angular gold frame and white face, this is one of the most elegant, refined, go-with-anything watches in the world. But it's no surprise, the Parisian luxury goods brand has all its watches made in its Swiss factory for the ultimate in quality.

JAEGER LECOULTRE REVERSO
Where? www.jaeger-lecoultre.com • Watches of Switzerland (see previous page)
How much? £7,900/$13,930/€11,560
Producers of the millionometre, a device that measures with an accuracy of one-thousandth of a millimetre, this brand dates back to 1931 and was originally produced for British army officers serving in India, who needed a watch to withstand hard knocks on the polo field. The elegant, angular gold Reverso is refined, luxurious and feminine.

Cartier Tankissme

AND THE AWARD FOR THE MOST EXPENSIVE WATCH EVER...
Goes to Vacheron Constantin, a Swiss company founded in 1755, which became famous for its intricate skeleton-style watches in which the wearer can see all the inner workings. The Kallista watch, named after the Greek word for 'most wonderful', was made from gold ingot and set with over 130 carats of emerald-cut diamonds. It took 8,700 hours to make and sold for £4 ($7.13) million.

Shoes & accessories

'I don't know who invented the high heel, but all women owe him a lot.'

Marilyn Monroe, actress, 1926–62

Belt

Gucci GG clasp green-red-green belt

Where?
Gucci stores worldwide • www.gucci.com
How much?
£135/$255/€195

Whether it's ultra-wide, super-skinny, studded or embossed, a well-made leather belt can transform a look in one easy fastening of its clasp. And if there's one belt that transcends styles, trends and eras, it is Gucci's classic GG belt in the brand's signature green-red-green colourway. Produced by craftsmen in Tuscany, this belt was worn by supermodels and entrepreneurs in the 1980s, preppy rich American kids in the 1990s, and suave Italians since the very beginning. It epitomizes a cool, laid-back luxury. You can wear it dressed-down with jeans and a tight T-shirt, or up with a prim pencil skirt and towering heels. The message: expensive, thoroughly grown-up and properly put-together.

HERMÈS H-CLASP BELT
Where? 24 Rue du Faubourg St Honoré, 75008, Paris, France • 00 33 1 40 17 47 17 • www.hermes.com
How much?
£245/$438/€358
What exactly is it about that sleek golden H? The classic Hermès leather belt has become a passport to instant chic. Just sling it round a pair of skinny jeans, a slim skirt or over mannish tailored trousers and it will add instant style and polish.

Gucci

BOTTEGA VENETA WOVEN LEATHER BELT
Where? Bottega Veneta stores worldwide • www.bottegaveneta.com
How much? £235/$400/€345
This classic Italian brand is famed for its high-quality lattice-woven leather, producing some of the most desirable belts in the world. Each belt is hand-tooled in Italy using the softest nappa leather known to man and woman.

Brogues

John Lobb

Where?

9 St James's Street, London, SW1 • 00 44 207 930 3664 • www.johnlobb.com •
Also sold in over 20 countries including France, USA and Japan

How much?

Bespoke brogues from £2,000/$3,555/€2,877

No other shoe has such classic appeal as a pair of finely crafted leather brogues, and nobody does them quite like John Lobb. Established in 1866, when Lobb designed a smart pair of riding boots for the Prince of Wales and was promptly awarded a royal warrant, the brand has since become a favourite with numerous well-heeled business men and celebrities, including Cecil Beaton, Somerset Maugham and more recently, Hugh Grant and Prince Charles, all of whom appreciate the classic style and superior craftsmanship.

John Lobb

Each pair is made from the finest leather, which is cut to the anatomical dimensions of the feet, while invisible details like full-grain leather insoles, linings and stiffeners add to the comfort of the shoes. The bespoke service at the elegant, wood-panelled London store is impeccable and starts off with a measurement by a fitter, who then makes up a wooden last of your foot. A 'clicker' helps decide on the exact leather, taking into consideration your requirements, and then sends the details to the company's Northampton factory, where the shoes are hand-sewn. It is an involved process and, depending on the style of the shoes and leather required, takes varying amounts of time; one of the most unusual leathers is alligator, which can take up to four skins – and three months – to ensure consistency in the grain and texture.

The most flattering brogue is Lobb's simple punched-toecap Oxford, the Philip II style. A mighty fine shoe and an investment for life, provided that you treat them with TLC.

BERLUTI
Where? 2 Rue du Pont-Neuf, 75001, Paris, France • 00 33 1 55 80 31 11 • www.berluti.com •
4 Harriet Street, London, SW1 • 00 44 207 823 23 00 • Stockists worldwide
How much? £2,200/$3,932/€3180
Berluti was established by an Italian woodmaker in Paris in 1895 and make sleek, refined brogues with a distinctly Continental aesthetic.

CHURCH'S
Where? 201 Regent Street, London, W1 • 00 44 207 734 2438 • www.churchsshoes.com
How much? From £270/$483/€390
A traditional British brand, specializing in good-quality ready-to-wear leather brogues.

'*Always use a shoehorn - it will help to keep your shoes in perfect shape. Walk your new shoes in gradually, wearing them for no more than a few hours and in dry conditions for the first few days. This allows the leather to soften and better fit your foot-shape. Rotate your pairs of shoes, so that they can dry out and breathe. If wet, leave your shoes to dry out naturally (never use an artificial heat source) on their sides so that air can circulate around both the upper and the sole. Generally, shoes will last longer if cared for properly and cleaned regularly.*'
Andres Hernandez, Production Manager at John Lobb

John Lobb

Clutch bag

Lulu Guinness fan

Where?

3 Ellis Street, London, SW1 • 00 44 207 823 4828 • www.luluguinness.com

How much?

From £395/$706/€579

'*B**are shoulders are a must for evening dresses and having a shoulder strap spoils the line, this is why a clutch bag is so good. As an accessories designer, I always make the bag the biggest statement of the outfit and shoes should complement but they certainly don't have to match. The worst look is when a woman wears a pale evening dress with a heavy dark quilted bag.*'

Lulu Guinness

It is neither the most fashion forward nor the most dazzling of clutch bags, but it is the most collectable, classic and utterly desirable, adored by glamazons that include Jemima Khan, Halle Berry and Sophie Dahl. Lulu Guinness' clutch fan combines humour with elegance and a dash of vintage glamour, reminiscent of old-style Hollywood. The British bag designer, who started her label in 1989 with a simple briefcase for ladies containing a bright suede lining, designed her first 'fan' bag in 1995, which subsequently sold out. Cleverly, Guinness only makes a limited number of bags, so each one becomes that much more unique and desirable. The 'fan' is a statement in its own right – you can wear the simplest of little black dresses and the elegant design will add a large dose of glamour and grace. Guinness' Crystal Fan (pictured), which originally sold for £775 ($1383), now sells on eBay for upwards of £1,000 ($1785).

Lulu Guinness

JUDITH LEIBER MINAUDIERE CRYSTAL CLUTCH

Where? Department stores worldwide • 680 Madison Avenue at 61st Street, New York, NY 10022 • 00 1 212 223 2999 • www.judithleiber.com

How much? From £1,051/$1,895/ €1,542

When Renée, Nicole and Scarlett are wondering which bag to take with them to their next red carpet event, there's no hesitation: a Judith Leiber minaudiere. Leiber's exquisite and expensive, gem-encrusted hard-case clutch bags spell all-out glamour.

VBH'S SATIN ENVELOP CLUTCH BAG

Where? www.brownsfashion.com

How much? £430/$750/€615

Rome-based and Florence-produced label, VBH (the initials of owner, V. Bruce Hoeksema, who used to work for Valentino) run a range of simple-but-striking envelop clutches that have acquired something of a cult following. Each bag is individually handcrafted and sewn by an intimate team in Florence, using the finest leathers. The signature rhodium-plated clasp makes this bag even more special.

Judith Leiber minaudiere crystal clutch, green

Judith Leiber minaudiere crystal clutch, spotted

WHERE TO BAG A VINTAGE CLUTCH

Until Coco Chanel invented the handbag in 1929, the clutch ruled supreme as the elegant choice for carting your compact, lipstick and other essentials around. This means there are lots of 1920s (and earlier) clutches to be found out there – it's just a matter of knowing where to look. In London, at the upper end of Portobello market (between Notting Hill Gate and Wesbourne Grove) there are some fabulous vintage bags stalls and accessory shops full of great clutches.

Alfies Antique market (12–25 Church Street, London, NW8) and Islington's Camden Passage (near the Angel tube station) are other options, while over in New York, regular antiques exhibition, Triple Pier Expo (www.stellashows.com), is a great place to pick up a gem of a clutch. In Paris, head to the flea market at Porte de Cligancourt (officially called Puces de Saint-Ouen), where you'll find clutch bags galore, dating back to the late 19th century among the numerous other interesting antiquities.

Cowboy boots

Texas Traditions

Where?
2222 College Ave, Austin, Texas, 78704 • 001 512 443
4447 • TexasTrad@aol.com

How much?
From £219/$400/€325

R Soles embroidered boot

For the wannabe, like *Midnight Cowboy*'s Joe Buck, the allure of a finely crafted pair of cowboy boots is practically narcotic. Dating back to mid-19th century Texas, the first cowboy boots were developed with a sturdy Cuban-style heel to grip in the stirrup. It wasn't until the 1920s that cowboy boots became a fashion accessory thanks to a number of fictional cowboy characters on the radio. The increased popularity of Western movies and the men who starred in them from the 1940s onwards – particularly the likes of John Wayne – only deepened the appeal of these boots. They've been in and out of fashion ever since – worn by stars as diverse as Lenny Kravitz, John Travolta and Tom Cruise, and more recently by female fashion icons like Sienna Miller (who popularized them with her modern bohemian look), Joss Stone and Britney Spears.

So, if you are an absolute cowboy boot fiend – and, let's face it, you either love them or loathe them – where do you go to find the best of the best? The answer is Texas Traditions, a company dating back over a hundred years. In 1937 it famously produced the most valuable cowboy boots ever; studded with diamonds, rubies and gold, they were designed for a high-profile gambler. Now owned by Lee Miller, who took over from Charlie Dunn, Texas Traditions still makes the best quality handcrafted leather cowboy boots in the world, which is why all the top country singers – and Sting – won't go anywhere else.

TONY LAMA

Where? Henry Beguelin, 18 Ninth Avenue, at 13th Street, inside Hotel Gansevoort, New York, NY 10014 •
00 1 212 647 8415 • www.tonylamabootshop.com • www.bootsbarn.com

How much? From about £137/$250/€250

A hundred production stages go into making a Tony Lama boot, which is constructed to fit a wide variety of sizes in a selection of skins that range from calf to ostrich. Each boot features a shank, a heavy gauge double-ribbed steel strip that supports the arch and is made to survive the rugged toughness of the high desert terrain around El Paso, where they are still handmade.

R SOLES

Where? 109a King's Road, London, SW3 • 00 44 207 351 5520 • www.rsolesboots.com

How much? From £195/$355/€289

Established by Douglas Berney on London's then-trendy Kings Road in 1975, R Soles quickly found a devout following of non-cowboys lusting after its fine quality cowboy boots. It remains one of the only independent shops along this famous street, offering the best cowboy boots you'll find in the UK. Designer Judy Rothchild has taken her styles to the catwalks of New York, London and Paris.

Eyeglasses

Frédéric Beausoleil

Where?
5 Bis Rue de l'Asile Popincourt, 75011, Paris, France • 00 33 1 42 77 28 29 • www.beausoleil.fr • Michael Guillon, 35 Duke of York Square, London, SW3

How much?
From £206/$365/€303

With the advent of laser surgery and contact lenses, wearing specs has become a little like listening to vinyl or using a fountain pen: an antiquated quirk that's not entirely necessary. Still, the die-hard spec wearer knows that a good pair of glasses can say a lot about image, appearance and status. Sure, there are modern alternatives, but somehow that takes the fun away from glasses, which are one of the few fashion accessories to fuse science with fashion and simultaneously symbolize intellectualism and professionalism. But where should you go for the ultimate pair?

Trained by an old spectacle manufacturer in Paris, Frédéric Beausoleil set out to design the most perfect glasses in the world. His label was established in 1987 and since then he's been selling his quality handmade frames to the likes of Al Pacino, Penelope Cruz and Julia Roberts, all of whom love his finely crafted signature rectangular frames.

GOLD & WOOD

Where? www.gold-and-wood.com • Michel Guillon, 35 Duke of York Square, London, SW3 • 00 44 207 730 2142

How much? From £350/$609/€510 Maurice Leonard started making a range of specs from fine wood frames in the early 1990s. In 1997, he pioneered the now-popular rimless look, and in 2001 he introduced the more luxurious Bijoux collection, which includes indulgent solid-gold frames inlaid with gemstones.

Frédéric Beausoleil

Alain Mikli's Starkeyes spectacles

ALAIN MIKLI STARKEYES

Where? 4 Rue Bachaumont, 75002, Paris, France • 00 33 1 44 82 08 42 • www.mikli.com

How much? From £1,000/$1,764/€1,463 for limited-edition frames

While not to everybody's taste, the thick, bold frames of Alain Mikli are instantly recognizable and spell confidence and style. His recent collaborations with designer Philippe Starck make for some of the most desirable specs going, due to the fact that they are resistant to air and water corrosion, twice as light as titanium and three-times lighter than steel.

THE WORLD'S BEST EYE BOUTIQUES

Adam Simmonds
87 Regents Park Road, London, NW1
00 44 207 813 1234 • www.adamsimmonds.co.uk

Anne et Valentin
4 Rue Sainte Croix de la Bretonnerie, 75004,
Paris, France
00 33 1 40 29 93 01 • www.anneetvalentin.com

Facial Index
1F Mitsubishi Denki Building, 2-2-3 Marunouchi,
Chiyoda-ku, Tokyo, Japan
00 813 5288 8220

Isis
153 Fulham Road, London, SW3
00 44 207 823 8080

Michel Guillon
35 Duke of York Square, Sloane Street, London, SW3
00 44 207 730 2142 • www.michelguillon.com

Niche Optical Tailor Ltd
119 Canleriggs, Glasgow, G1 1NP, Scotland
00 44 141 553 2077

Robert Marc
575 Madison Avenue, New York, NY 10022
001 212 319 2000

AND WEBSITES...

www.klasik.org
www.olivergoldsmith.com
www.retrospecs.co.uk: you can commission the
same style of specs Audrey Hepburn wore in the
1966 *How to Steal a Million* for £400!

Fountain Pen

Mont Blanc Meisterstück 149

Where?

www.montblanc.com •

Various branches and distributors worldwide, including: The Fountain Pen Hospital, 10 Warren Street, New York, NY 10007 • 00 1 212 964 0580 • www.fountainpenhospital.com

How much?

Approximately £335/$588/€489

Mont Blanc Meisterstück 149

The Mont Blanc Solitaire Royal pen, which is encrusted with 4,810 diamonds, is the most expensive pen ever at £70,000 ($125,000). Of course there are far cheaper alternatives – but Mont Blanc remains the brand with the most cachet.

The company was founded in Germany in 1906 and was innovative from the start, making special fountain pens with blades instead of nibs for architects and engineers during the 1920s. But its most popular style is the Meisterstück, in particular the chubby, cigar-shaped 149 model. The pen is utterly iconic and instantly recognizable – so much so that it is now on permanent display at New York's Museum of Modern Art. The Meisterstück was first introduced in 1924, and famous users include JFK and most of the recent Popes.

Made of black resin with a gold trim, the cap is topped with a signature Mont Blanc white star, a motif that represents the snow-covered summit of Mont Blanc itself. The nib is equally special, made from 18 carat gold with a platinum inlay. Each 149 passes through the hands of 120 people during its three-month production process, which includes checking the sound it makes when it hits paper and writing enough figure-of-eights to fill an A4 page. Mont Blanc has resolutely resisted the urge to use cartridges and so pens must still be filled with ink from a bottle.

The torpedo size might feel unwieldy in smaller hands; thankfully, the Meisterstück also comes in smaller sizes, all made with the same design values – the 'Classique' is a popular example. When pen shopping, you should try as many styles as possible to discover which you find most comfortable.

PARKER 51

Where? Vintage pen specialists, including: www.penfriend.co.uk • www.penhome.com • www.fountainpenhospital.com

How much? Depending on colourway, date, cap style and condition, from £50/$88/€73

Everyone from the composer Puccini to thousands of school children the world over has used a Parker pen. The most covetable model of this American brand is the Parker 51, introduced in 1941; like the Mont Blanc Meisterstück, it can be found in New York's Museum of Modern Art.

DUPONT ORPHEO

Where? 58 Avenue Montaigne, 75008, Paris, France • 00 33 1 53 91 30 00 • www.st-dupont.com

How much? Approximately £305/$535/€445

Perhaps the most elegant range on the market, France's answer to Mont Blanc uses lush Chinese lacquers to coat their pens. Their limited editions are well worth seeking out.

> '**M**y two fingers on a typewriter have never connected with my brain. My hand on a pen does. A fountain pen, of course. Ballpoint pens are only good for filling out forms on a plane.'
>
> Graham Greene, writer

Gloves

Madova

Where?

Via Guicciardini, Florence 50125, Italy • 00 39 05 52 39 65 26 • www.madova.com

How much?

From £31/$59/€43

Asmart pair of leather gloves is the best way to finish off a winter coat. A family firm that was founded in Florence in 1919, Madova claims to be the only shop in Europe, and quite possibly the world, that sells and produces leather gloves – and nothing else.

Madova's strong point is variety – visit the shop and you can find a glove in virtually every colour under the sun, at any length, both unlined and lined in wool, silk, cashmere and the warmest – albeit least animal-friendly – rabbit fur. Helpful assistants will find you the correct size; new gloves should be tight-fitting as they'll stretch with the shape of your hand. The staff will also present you with a handy booklet detailing tips on how to care for and clean your gloves. For the ultimate in glove luxury, plump for the made-to-measure option, which is also surprisingly affordable – around £35 ($62) for kidskin leather lined with silk.

Madova

AGNELLE

Where? www.agnelle.fr • www.brownsfashion.com

How much? From £65/$117/€95

This Paris-based company makes gloves for Louis Vuitton, Christian Dior, Lanvin and Celine, as well as producing its own line. Best known for stylish designs with a twist – think tassel details and bows resting on the wrist.

PICKETT

Where? 32–33 and 41 Burlington Arcade, London, W1 • 00 44 207 493 8939 • www.pickett.co.uk

How much? From £57.50/$103/€84

Pickett is best for gloves in bold colours – the gorgeous hues it uses include fire-engine red and raspberry pink. Styles include lined, unlined, three-quarter-length and short. Particularly recommended are the gentlemen's cape leather 'Officers' gloves, with delicious details such as a red silk lining and a button fastening on the wrist.

Handbag

Hermès Birkin

Where?
Hermès stores worldwide •
www.hermes.com
How much?
From £3,500/$5,148/€6,445

Hermès Birkin

Right now having a designer handbag is more important than possessing a designer dress – the 'it' bag is the fashion phenomenon of the 21st century. And while the world's chicest women will happily shop at Zara for clothes, there's no way they'll compromise when it comes to their bag – it must be as covetable and lust-worthy as can be. If there's one bag that always outshines the competition, it is the Hermès Birkin. Loved by Kate Moss, Madonna and Elle MacPherson alike, it still garners waiting lists of three months or more. The actress, Jane Birkin, inspired the creation of the first of these bags in 1984 – a supple black leather carry-all, which knocked the Kelly from the top spot due to its larger size. Now available in a variety of different sizes, including the popular shoulder style, which features a longer handle, the Birkin can be ordered in 8,000 different combinations of leather and fastenings. The most exclusive and expensive style ever? Perhaps the black crocodile Birkin, customized with a clasp and lock and featuring 14 carats of pavé diamonds set in white gold, which recently sold at auction in New York for a cool £35,500 ($64,800). If you want one, remortgage your house now.

Chanel 2.55

CHANEL 2.55
Where? Chanel stores worldwide • www.chanel.com
How much? From £800/$1,473/€1,173
It was 1929 when Coco Chanel first designed the shoulder bag; until then the clutch had ruled as the choice of elegant handbag for women, and soldiers' satchels were the only bags with straps. Chanel declared: 'I am tired of carrying my bag in my hand and losing it, so one day I added a strap and wore it as a shoulder bag.'

By 1955, she'd developed a quilted chain-strap bag, now referred to affectionately as the 'quilt and guilt', which she named the 2.55, after its birthdate – February 1955.

MULBERRY BAYSWATER

Where? Mulberry stores worldwide • www.mulberry.com
How much? £495/$911/€728

A simple, practical and quintessentially British design, this leather holdall became an instant hit when it was developed by Mulberry in 2003. The brand was established in the 1970s by Roger Saul and has become something of a cult bag label ever since. Luella Bartley hooked up with them in 2001 to create the famous Gisele bag. Now, under the Creative Direction of Stuart Ververs, Mulberry looks set to reign as a traditional but forward-thinking British brand, and its roomy Bayswater will no doubt go down as an all-time classic.

Mulberry Bayswater

A SHORT HISTORY OF THE 'IT' BAG

1932 Louis Vuitton Noé In signature monogram canvas, this was one of the very first cult handbags, thanks to its practical drawstring and elegant strap.

1944 LL Bean Tote Before fridges were commonly used, US brand LL Bean introduced the 'Ice Carrier' made from heavy duty canvas. It was renamed the 'Boat & Tote' in the 1960s as it became increasingly fashionable.

1958 Hermès Kelly Bag A hit when it launched in the late 1950s, this Hermès bag was renamed after Grace Kelly after she carried it around throughout her engagement to Prince Rainier. The Kelly still garners three-month long waiting lists.

1965 Gucci's 'Jackie' Shoulder Bag Simple in shape: a curved leather body with a Gucci clasp and curved shoulder strap, this bag fits snugly under the arm and became the must-have bag of the 1960s.

1996 Hervé Chapelier Travelbags These French holdalls with signature contrasting interior and exterior waterproof nylon canvas became a fashion statement during the mid to late 1990s.

1993 Kate Spade Tote The most simple of concepts: a durable, simple-shaped nylon tote that became one of the most unlikely – and best selling – accessory style hits in the US in the 1990s.

1999 Fendi Baguette A frenzy began soon after Fendi launched its now legendary baguette bag in the late 1990s. The fight was on to find ever new and more embellished versions, whether mirrored, sequin-scattered or appliquéd.

2001 Christian Dior Saddle Bag A small shoulder bag in the shape of a saddle with the all-important C and D in chunky silver dangling from the strap, this was a hit with the international jet-set crowd.

2002 Luella Gisele In simple tan, this satchel-inspired bag with buckles and straps became an instant best seller for Mulberry. Luella then launched many new variations on the theme under her own label, Luella. These came in different shapes and colours, including bubble-gum pink.

2003 Balenciaga City Motocycle This neat handheld leather bag's defining feature was its wispy leather tassles. Kate Moss carried hers everywhere she went for a while and the supermodel's patronage helped to propel it to the height of style stardom.

2005 Chloê Paddington The slouchy leather bag with its signature weighty gold padlock shot to the top of the must-have bag super league the moment it was launched. A smaller, more compact version soon followed.

Luggage

Louis Vuitton

Where?
Louis Vuitton stores worldwide • www.vuitton.com

How much?
From £430/$764/€631 for a monogram hold-all

The two most important jobs of a suitcase? First, to hold your clothes neatly and safely, and second to look so refined that you will have fellow travellers drooling in the baggage reclaim hall. There is no contest when choosing which will garner the biggest drools: a Louis Vuitton classic monogrammed trunk. The label, established in 1854 with the creation of its flat trunk (which remains the classiest style) has been selling its Damier canvases since 1888, and the iconic monogrammed canvas since 1896, to the super rich from Posh and Becks to British royalty. But what, exactly, is the attraction with these cases? Perhaps the simplicity of the logo? The subdued gold and brown colourway? Or the chic gold clasps? It is probably a combination of all three, but there is no doubt about it: Vuitton's classic LV monogrammed canvas trunks are the most luxurious, expensive and, let's face it, ostentatious, luggage sets in the world.

Louis Vuitton trunk

GLOBE TROTTER

Where? 54–55 Burlington Arcade, London, W1 • 00 44 207 529 5952 • www.globe-trotterltd.com • For the unique bespoke cases: 00 44 207 529 5950 or email bespoke@globe-trotterltd.com

How much? £155/$279/€217

Established in 1897, the Globe Trotter, with its old-fashioned charm, is the archetypal English suitcase. They are made from Vulcan Fibre, a unique, patented material that is as light as aluminium but as hardwearing as the finest leather, and thus rather brilliantly last a lifetime. Each piece is lovingly hand-crafted at the company's Hertfordshire factory by the same machines that were used in the early 1900s. Globe Trotter now offers a bespoke service that invites clients to choose from a selection of colours, exclusive Liberty-print linings, contrasting leather corners and personalized initialling.

Globe Trott[er] customize[d] suitcase

Globe Trotter

BOTTEGA VENETA RUBBERIZED CANVAS CARRY-ALLS

Where? www.bottegaveneta.com

How much? £1,521/$2,800/€2,239

These durable cases from the luxury Italian label feature shoe pockets, leather straps to ensure your belongings are fastened in safely, leather address tags and brass locking hardware. They are available in stylish brown with a black trim or black with a tan trim.

**HOW TO PACK WITHOUT CREASING:
GARRY CHARNOCK, BRAND MANAGER
FOR JEEVES OF BELGRAVIA
(WWW.JEEVESOFBELGRAVIA.CO.UK)**

• How you fold your garments is very important. Make sure that you fold your clothes around the body pulse points – believe it or not the body heat generated around the bend of the knee, the wrists and elbows will help steam out the creases in your items when you wear them.

• Pack shoes toe to heel in the bags they arrive in.

• Jersey – do not fold, just roll and then unravel for minimum creasing (this will also act as a stabiliser to fill any spaces).

• Pleated skirts and dresses – twist the pleat and pull it into a stocking to maintain the pleat.

• Double bag all cosmetics to avoid spillage in your suitcase. Ideally, take all your cosmetics in a vanity case to protect them from damage.

• Always take laundry bags.

• Take a large canvas holdall if you intend to shop.

Make-up bag

Pucci

Where?
Pucci stores worldwide • www.pucci.com
How much?
From £60/$110/€90

Pucci

A make-up bag is the one thing most women use every day. It needs to fit in your handbag, look good on your dressing table, and impress at those moments when you whip it out in the bathroom at a wedding or wild party. The perfect bag must also be big enough to fit in the five essentials: compact, lipstick, eyeliner, mascara and blusher. But above all it should make a statement. And no brand is better at bold statement making than Pucci, the exotic Italian print label, established in 1951 and famous for its colourful swirly prints that were originally based on medieval Italian banners. One of its signature make-up bags will gain more than a few envious glances.

Penhaligon's

PENHALIGON'S

Where? 20a Brook Street, London, W1 • 00 44 207 493 0002 • www.penhaligons.co.uk
How much? £35/$64/€52
In the late 1860s, William Henry Penhaligon left his native Penzance in the picturesque south-west of England, and came to London to establish himself as a barber, supplying perfumes, toilet waters and pomades to the aristocracy. Today, Penhaligon's range includes quality leather make-up bags, including the nappa leather half-moon style, which is available in a palette of seasonal colours. Each piece is exquisitely crafted and presented in a luxurious pouch and box.

Liberty

LIBERTY

Where? Regent Street, London, W1 • 00 44 207 734 1234 • www.liberty.co.uk
How much? From £10/$20/€17
From the fine-scale, dainty, floral design known simply as the 'Liberty Print' to the intricate and ornate Tana Lawn, Liberty's classic fabrics make for the sweetest make-up bags a girl can get.

Sandals

K Jacques

Where?
25 Rue Allard, 83990 Saint Tropez, France • 00 33 4 94 97 38 67 • www.lestropeziennes.com

How much?
£136/$245/€200

K Jacques

Sandals may be the simplest form of footwear, but there's a huge difference between the kind you buy for a fiver on the high street and the hand-tooled leather variety, which are properly fitted to your feet and can be found in Europe's most exclusive resorts. The ideal sandal should transport you from beach to cocktail party; it should be elegant, yet practical, and show your feet off in the best possible way – complementing a tan and distracting attention from chubby chipolata toes.

The most famous and adored sandal shop in the world, the K Jacques store in St Tropez, was established in 1933 by Monsieur and Madame Jacques Kéklikian. It was a shrewd business move: in St Tropez, sandals are as much a necessity as jeans and a white T-shirt. Their new style of made-to-measure sandals swiftly granted them a celebrity following and in the 1960s the shop shod the soles of Brigitte Bardot. Today the firm is still a family business and has three sales outlets in St Tropez, as well as a showroom that creates sandals for a wide range of the world's leading designers, including Karl Lagerfeld, Missoni and Helmut Lang. With a choice of over 200 styles, you can get any shape, style or colour made up with a special bespoke service that takes just a few hours. The only additional requirement is an immaculate pedicure.

AMEDEO CANFORA 'JASMINE' JEWELLED THONG

Where? 3 Via Camerelle, near Piazzetta Quisisana, Capri, Italy • 00 39 081 837 0487 • www.canfora.com

How much? £150/$270/€220

Founded by Amedo Canfora in 1946, this company is now looked after by his daughters Angela and Rita. Situated on the glitzy Italian island of Capri, this sandal shop dishes out elegant sandals to well-dressed holiday makers, from models to fashion designers, all of whom adore the handmade, jewelled, thong designs. Elegant, glamorous and distinctly Italian.

Amedeo Canfora 'Jasmine' jewelled thong

STAVROS MELISSINOS 'SOPHIA LOREN' LEATHER CORD SANDALS

Where? Melissinos Art, 2 Aghias Theklas, Athens, Greece • 00 3 210 321 9247 • www.melissinos-art.com

How much? From £15/$27/€20

A poet and sandal maker who has been tooling both words and leather for more than 50 years, Melissinos has made shoes for both Sophia Loren and the Beatles. His 15 types of sandal can be adjusted to fit as you wait.

Scarf

Duchamp

Where?
Liberty, Regent Street, London, W1 • 00 44 207 734 1234 • www.liberty.co.uk
How much?
From £100/$178/€147

Men's scarves have a huge and varied history: they are evident on ancient Chinese sculptures; the Romans later wore something called a sudarium, which was a linen kerchief; and in 17th-century Britain, no man would be seen dead without an elegant silk scarf. Widening and protecting the neck, it was considered to reinforce masculinity and was adopted by women much later on. Recently the silk scarf has made something of a comeback, along with bespoke suits, brogues and silk socks. A silk scarf is gentlemanly, luxurious and a sign of total refinement. Duchamp men's accessory label has a selection of the most delightful gentleman's silk scarves in vibrant prints and colours.

Duchamp

TOOTAL
Where? Selfridges, 400 Oxford Street, London, W1 • 00 44 8708 377 377 • www.selfridges.com • for more stockists ring 00 44 1788 575 800
How much? From £35/$65/€52
This recently relaunched iconic British brand was favoured by the 'Mods' in the 1960s, who wore its tassle-trimmed scarves with their parkas.

ETRO
Where? 14 Old Bond St, London, W1 • 00 44 207 495 5767 • www.etro.it
How much? From £150/$264/€221
The Italian fashion brand famous for its colourful paisley prints does fine silk scarves for men, including coloured pashminas.

Slippers

Pia Wallén

Where?

From selected stockists such as Skandium, www.skandium.com. For more information, visit www.piawallen.se

How Much?

£37/$67/€54

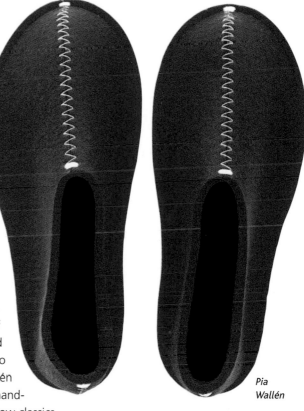

Pia Wallén

Coming from a place where it's dark most of the year, the Scandinavians know a thing or two about comfort. They also know a thing or two about style, making Pia Wallén's wool felt slippers the best when it comes to keeping your toes toasty.

Wallén is an award-winning Stockholm-based interior designer who started working in high-quality felt – and never really wavered. Her slippers are made from just that, with contrasting zig-zag stitching across the toe and rubber soles, available in a number of pleasingly bright colourways and styles. The full-footed affair, for instance, is perfect for the kind of people who don't want their slippers to look like, well, slippers. Wallén also makes a range of rugs, blankets, pillows – her hand-woven wool throws with a cross motif, 'The Crux', are now classics.

And while we're on the subject of slipper shopping in chilly climes, super-warm Mongolian slip-ons made from yak leather and camel hair also come highly recommended.

BELDI BABOUCHES

Where? Beldi, 9–11 Souikat Laksour, Medina, Marrakech, Morocco • 00 212 44 441 076

How much? £43/$79/€63

Moroccan babouches are *the* smart slipper choice. The pointy-toed version was invented in the Moroccan city of Fez, where distinctive yellow and white slippers are still made today for the royal household. Those with a rounder toe - less severe and more aesthetically pleasing - are from Marrakech, the smartest from Beldi, a boutique that flawlessly blends oriental craftsmanship with occidental taste. Beldi's babouches are more expensive than most but worth it since they're hand-sewn in the finest leather. Jean Paul Gaultier is a fan – he has a riad in the old medina – as are many of his fellow fashion jetsetters.

SHEEPSKIN SCUFFS

Where? www.celtic-sheepskin.co.uk • www.hush-uk.com

How much? £29/$52/€42

From the same brain that brought you the Ugg boot, scuffs are crafted from soft suede with a toe-pleasing sheepskin lining. Perfect for chilly winter's nights when only sheepskin will do.

Socks

Pantherella

Where?
www.pantherella.co.uk
How much?
Approximately £11/$19/€16 per pair

For many men, socks are something of a trademark. Think about it: booted and suited, how else are they going to stand out from the corporate crowd? Pantherella, a company based in Leicester, has been going for over 65 years and is generally considered the best sock-maker in the world – if you're buying your suit from Savile Row, Pantherella is where you'll get your socks.

Pantherella

The company's founder, Louis Goldschmidt, established a fine-gauge knitting plant after spotting a trend towards lightweight clothing. Even today, Pantherella insists on using only the highest-quality yarns – cashmere, silk, and merino wool, for instance, as well as its bestselling line in Sea Island cotton. Pantherella has exclusive rights to make socks from genuine Sea Island cotton, so, unlike 'Sea Island quality', which is used by many of their competitors, this is the real deal – it's as strong as silk, as soft as cashmere and as long-lasting as wool; cool in summer, warm in winter.

Pantherella's other claim to fame is the socks' hand-linked toe seam, a skilled process that other sock manufacturers have rejected as too expensive. The process creates an invisible toe seam, which means increased comfort for the wearer. As for the correct sock etiquette, Savile Row tailors decree that no skin should be shown between the sock and trouser leg when sitting down.

BURLINGTON ARGYLE SOCKS
Where? www.figleaves.com • www.sockshop.co.uk • All good department stores
How much? Approximately £7/$13/€10
Burlington make the best brightly coloured argyle socks, which come complete with trademark stud. They're so good, in fact, that they even used the 13th Duke of Argyle in one of their advertising campaigns – the diamond pattern is based on the Argyle tartan.

GAMMARELLI
Where? Via dei Cestari, Rome, Italy • www.vivre.com
How much? Approximately £6/$11/€9
This shop is known as 'the Pope's couturier', as the boutique, which was established in 1798, has dressed virtually every Pope since then. It is best for bright cardinal-red socks, which are ribbed and come to the knee – some men have a fetish about such things. Also available in Archbishop Purple.

Stilettos

Manolo Blahnik

Where?
49-51 Old Church Street, London,
SW3 • 00 44 207 352 8622
How much?
From £375/$690/€552

Manolo Blahnik

M adonna once described Manolo Blahnik's shoes as 'better than sex', adding 'what's more, they last longer'. She has a point. In an average lifetime, a woman spends up to three years of her life shopping, shelling out £31,680 on shoes. Is it any wonder, then, that the search for the perfect pair of stilettos is so vital?

Manolo Blahnik is a man who knows all about this and his shoes have become legendary for their ability to turn a woman into a sex siren within seconds of stepping in to them. Blahnik, who was born to a Spanish mother and Czech father and raised on a banana plantation in the Canary Islands, studied literature at the University of Geneva and art at the Ecole du Louvre in Paris. During a trip to New York, he had an appointment with the then editor of American *Vogue*, Diana Vreeland, who encouraged him to settle in London and set up his shoe label.

A QUICK Q&A WITH MANOLO BLAHNIK

Why does a stiletto heel change the way a woman looks so dramatically?
Manolo Blahnik: 'I adore the way a woman's body changes when she puts on heels; it is an instant transformation, no surgery necessary! From a technical point of view, when you raise the heel it forces the body to work completely differently.'

How does it alter her attitude?
MB: 'Shoes are always instant theatre, they help a person act who they want to be.'

When is a strap good? Any rules?
MB: 'Every single woman's legs are completely different and luckily there are endless options for straps. As a rule, an ankle strap will cut your leg, making it appear shorter, so if your legs are proportionately short, I would advise against straps. Each person must try everything on to find what works best for them.'

When should stilettos be worn?
MB: 'ALWAYS!'

When shouldn't stilettos be worn?
MB: 'If you are visiting an apartment or house with exquisite 18th-century parquet flooring.'

Your first memory of stilettos?
MB: 'Possibly my mother in shoes of her own design.'

Your favourite stiletto wearer of all time and why?
MB: 'Women in general!'

It is lucky for the women of the world that he did. From the outset of his career, Blahnik has had an instinct for proportion that has placed him above his competitors; his stilettos miraculously lengthen the leg from the hip right down to the tip of the toe and his classic shapes and styles are never overtly fashionable, remaining timelessly stylish. And while every celebrity from Nicole Kidman to Kylie Minogue has stepped out in a pair of Manolos, it is good old Marge Simpson, who wore a pair of his mules during a 1991 episode of *The Simpsons*, and, of course, *Sex and the City*'s Carrie Bradshaw, who symbolize exactly how culturally significant a pair of Manolo stilettos really are.

Manolo Blahnik

CHRISTIAN LOUBOUTIN

Where? 23 Motcomb Street, London, SW1 • 00 44 207 245 6510

How much? From £375/$690/€552

This French designer is known for his slim, vertiginous pencil-like heels with signature Chinese-red soles that have prompted men to follow women down the street upon seeing a flash of scarlet. Louboutin, who was inspired to become a shoe designer at the age of ten after spying a woman in an art gallery wearing the most striking pair of heels, says his shoes are 'a worktool or a weapon and an objet d'art'. As well as producing two collections of drop-dead sexy shoes a year, he works on private commissions – love letters and locks of hair are among the things that have been encased in those spiky, conical, wicked heels of his.

Christian Louboutin

The best shoe-a-holic website

www.shoewawa.com is a comprehensive website for shoe lovers, covering news on the latest brands and styles, as well as the newest eBay offerings so you know all about that must-have pair of Manolos or Ferragamo Mary-Janes selling for pennies. It also features many specialist categories, including 'ugly shoes', 'design classics' and 'wedges'. A must for shoe-addicts everywhere.

HISTORY OF THE STILETTO

The inventive shoe designer, Salvatore Ferragamo, created the reinforced steel bar that gave rise to the stiletto heel in the 1950s. But it was French shoe designer Roger Vivier who took it one step further in the following decades, fully realizing the potential of the stiletto as an iconic heel shape. The stiletto heel is now one of the most stylish and important heel shapes in existence and features not only in exclusive designer shoe collections, but across the high street too.

Rupert Sanderson

RUPERT SANDERSON

Where? 33 Bruton Place, London, W1 • 00 44 870 750 9181 • www.rupertsanderson.co.uk
How much? From about £340/$600/€495
After training at Cordwainers, British shoe designer Rupert Sanderson worked for Sergio Rossi in Italy before setting up his own label in Mayfair in 2001. His beautifully made, elegant heels with a dash of frivolity have fast been garnering a fanbase among the world's serious shoephiles, including Scarlett Johansson.

Sunglasses

Ray-Ban

Where?
www.raybansunglasses.co.uk •
Department stores
worldwide •
www.luxottica.com

How much?
£59/$104/€86

More than merely functional, sunglasses signify status, wealth and, above all else, image. One of the most iconic styles is the classic Ray-Ban Aviator. Army Air Corps commissioned Bausch & Lamb to design the teardrop-shaped Aviator in 1936 out of necessity – pilots had been suffering from headaches and nausea because of glare and the great distances they needed to travel. The name 'Ray-Ban' was chosen for the new product to emphasize the fact that the eyewear could 'ban' or block out the sun's rays and protect the wearer's eyes. In 1952, Ray-Ban launched a new model, the Wayfarer, a style that was promptly snapped up by Hollywood stars, including Audrey Hepburn, who wore a pair in *Breakfast at Tiffany's*. The Aviator was popularized again in the 1980s, when Tom Cruise wore them in *Top Gun*. To this day, Ray-Bans, recently enjoying a renaissance, remain chic and timeless.

Ray-Ban

Boucheron

BOUCHERON
Where? 26 Place Vendôme, 75001, Paris, France • 00 33 1 42 61 58 16 • 164 New Bond Street, London, W1 • 00 44 207 514 9170 • www.boucheron.com

Boucheron

How much? £339/$600/€499

You can't get a 'blingier' pair of shades than Boucheron's. With a simple wrap-around shape and crystal-encrusted B on the hinge of each arm, they're sure to garner a few raised eyebrows on the beach.

OLIVER PEOPLES' CAMEO

Where? www.oliverpeoples.com • Oliver Peoples stores in the US and Japan • Selected opticians worldwide

How much? £139/$245/€203

A simple Jackie O-style, Oliver Peoples' Cameo comes in a selection of colours, including the most stylish of purple hues. This LA brand, established in 1986, has fast become the favoured brand of celebrities, including Kate Moss, who has made them famous by wearing them absolutely everywhere. Oliver Peoples have all the rock and roll credentials with none of the show of the more well-known brands.

WHICH STYLES SUIT WHICH FACE SHAPES BY TOP OPTOMETRIST, MICHEL GUILLON

- **Round (soft, no angular features).**
  Go for: contrast by adding feature: rectangular/hexagonal frames.
- **Rectangular (marked and more balanced features, as a square face, but not as wide)**
  Go for: softer shape, oval to soften the image.
- **Triangular (like a rectangular face but with narrow chin).**
  Go for: small non-angular eye shape to minimize the difference in head width between the eye region and chin.
- **Square (broad face with strong jaw and chin).**
  Go for: rectangular elliptical frame with rounded softer corners.
- **Oval (soft regular features).**
  Go for: the choice is yours, with any style you wish: discreet to minimize contrast or bold to maximize impact.

Say it with shades

- **Bottega Veneta:** For Milanese-style chic.
- **Chanel:** If only because of those tiny interlocking Cs on each side.
- **Dior:** Heir- and heiress-glamour, think Paris Hilton.
- **Roberto Cavalli:** The choice of the footballer and his wife for maximum show.
- **Yves Saint Laurent:** Refined with a dash of opulence.

Trainers

Adidas Superstar

Where?
www.adidas.com •
Sports stores
worldwide
How much?
From £60/$109/€89

Adidas Superstar

Without doubt, the most iconic trainer – or sneaker – is the Adidas Superstar. This model first went on sale in 1970 and recently celebrated its 35th anniversary. Initially worn by NBA players, it fast transcended to the street. In 1986, US hip-hop band, Run DMC, released the track 'My Adidas' and threw away the laces. There's something almost personable about the chubby round toe, the short, smart shoe shape and the thick laces that make it aesthetically appealing and as comfy as can be.

Nike Air Max 90s

NIKE AIR MAX 90S
Where? www.nike.com • Selected sports stores worldwide
How much? From £70/$128/€104

One of Nike's two founders, Phil Knight, was a middle-distance runner at the University of Oregon and established Nike in the early 1970s, naming it after the Greek winged goddess. The brand, which was the first to launch the clever concept of limited editions, came up with the Air Max design in 1987 – it displayed the all-important air bubble sole prominently and became a cult-classic in 1988 with this sleek and simple design. The Air Max continues to be re-released in updated versions each season.

REEBOK CLASSICS
Where? www.rbk.com • Selected sports stores worldwide
How much? From £50/$91/€74

'Let's put on our Classics and have a little dance shall we?' sings The Streets' Mike Skinner, the recent face of Reebok Classics. So what's the draw of these most plain of trainers? First released in 1987, they're one of the biggest selling trainer styles in the UK. Simple lines, mostly white and unpretentious in shape and style, the Reebok Classic has an urban coolness that has made it the trainer of choice for the casual – DJ and East-end builder alike. Its strength is the simplicity of its design, which makes them so easy to wear and appealing to everyone. A timeless classic.

Reebok Classics

Umbrella

Swaine Adeney Brigg

Where?
54 St James, London, SW1 • 00 44 207 409 7277
www.swaineadeney.co.uk

How much?
£2700/$4918/€4011

Swaine Adeney Brigg

For the discerning gentleman, an umbrella is not just for keeping the rain off, but is a telling status symbol. Umbrellas may have been used in China and India for thousands of years before they ended up in England in the 18th century, but there's no doubt that the UK is now home to the best-quality umbrellas in the world. Swaine Adeney Brigg is as old-fashioned a company as they come. Originating in 1836, it has been making umbrellas for the British royal family ever since. Its history is diverse, supplying luggage to Rolls Royce, Aston Martin and Bentley, and bullwhips for Indiana Jones in *Raiders of the Lost Ark*.

When it comes to umbrellas, the company's signature pieces include the Brigg Malacca umbrella handle, fashioned from Malaysian Mallaca cane, but the ultimate in luxury is the ebonized wood umbrella. There is also a ladies' parasol with a rhino horn handle, a snip at just £1,200. You wouldn't want to be leaving that on the tube now, would you?

JAMES SMITH & SON

Where? 53 New Oxford St, London, WC1 • 00 44 207 836 4731
How much? £525/$780/€956

James Smith & Son has been a shrine to the umbrella since the 1850s. There is a bespoke service that allows you to choose the wood and colour you desire, as well as measuring the umbrella so that it is the right length when you walk. The elegant rosewood style is a fine-looking specimen.

James Smith & Son

PICKETT

Where? 32–33 Burlington Arcade, London, W1 • 00 44 207 493 8939 •
www.pickett.co.uk
How much? £169/$308/€251

This quality English leather accessories label offers a beautiful classic Malacca-handled umbrella. The epitome of understated British refinement.

Budget brollies

If the thought of spending upwards of £100 on an umbrella makes you sweat, go for a more practical foldaway option. A telltale sign of a good umbrella is the quality and quantity of rivets in the frame – make sure there are lots of them and that they are secure and well-made. One of the best foldaway umbrellas is the Knirp Duomatic Fiber T1. It features a carbonfibre frame and it is rust-proof and apparently storm-proof. It is available at James Smith & Son (see above).

Wallet

Connolly

Where?

Connolly, 41 Conduit Street, London, W1 •
00 44 207 235 3883

How much?

From £99/$182/€147

A wallet is one of the most practical and important accessories there is: where else can you put all those platinum credit cards and cash? If you're looking for a suitably stylish wallet, then look no further than Connolly, the quintessentially English luxury brand that is famous for its fine quality leather goods. Connolly has produced some of the world's best leather, which has been used on the first ever Rolls Royce, Edward VII's coronation coach, Concorde and the QE2. The company dates back some 200 years, when James Connolly built a small business as a tyresmith. Since then Connolly leather has been used to fashion the boots of British soldiers in the First World War, on the seats on London buses, on the first tube trains and in approximately 14 parliaments around the world, including the Palace of Westminster. No wonder Ralph Lauren is a huge fan.

Connolly

MULBERRY

Where? 41–42 New Bond Street, London, W1 • 00 44 207 491 3900 •
www.mulberry.co.uk

How much? £99/$182/€147

Another great British brand, Mulberry produces some of the most desirable leather accessories in the world, including its classic faux tortoise-skin leather wallets. The company was established in the 1970s in rural Somerset, where it remains today, and still employs local craftsmen and artisans. The accessories marry style and function, so they not only look good but feel great too. The classic wallet features an ample slot for four credit cards, a coin section, two hidden compartments and a cash sleeve.

Mulberry

GOYARD

Where? 233 Rue Saint Honoré, 75001, Paris, France •
00 33 1 42 60 57 04 • www.goyard.fr

How much? From £50/$91/€74

Believe it or not, this French luxury luggage brand, established in 1853, was once bigger than Louis Vuitton and was the first of the two companies to introduce coated canvas printed with its signature pattern – it still produces fabulous steamer trunks and luxury pet accessories, by the way. A wallet with the classic Goyard chevrons, which are always hand-painted on, is a subtle sign of style. An insider's secret.

Leisure

*'They talk of the dignity of work.
The dignity is in leisure.'*

*Herman Melville,
American novelist and poet,
1819—1891*

Bicycle

Pashley Princess Sovereign

Where?
Pashley Cycles, Stratford-upon-Avon, Warwickshire, CV37 9NL • 00 44 1789 292 263 • www.pashley.co.uk

How much?
£495/$896/€547

First invented by Thomas Humber in 1868, bicycles are bound up in childhood memories: we all remember the first time the stabilizers came off and the joy of pedalling freely. Buying a bicycle is in many ways a more personal and sentimental process than buying a car or a scooter. And while there are thousands of high-tech, super-modern bikes in all sorts of shapes and sizes, none have the romance, history or aesthetic delights of William Pashley's elegant and traditional ladies' bicycles. Lovingly handmade for over 70 years in Stratford-upon-Avon, this quintessentially English bicycle features a front basket, five-speed alloy hub gears and a Brooks leather saddle with springs that mould to your bottom. The Princess Sovereign, available in Regency Green, Buckingham Black, or Rich Burgundy, is stylish, classic and a pleasure to ride.

Pashley Princess Sovereign

SCHWINN CRUISERS
Where? www.schwinnbike.com
How much? £305/$549.99/€447
Founded in the United States in 1895, Schwinn was one of the original purveyors of the modern bicycle. The company has since brought us many classic bikes, including the stylized Sting-Ray – with its high-rise handlebars, 'banana' seat and enlarged back wheel – in 1963, and the BMX in 1970. Its fabulously lightweight Whitewall Typhoon cruiser tyre is the original smooth roller for easy riding, featuring corrosion-resistant alloy wheels and stainless-steel spokes. The Cruiser has classic, curvy, 1950s' styling and a two-tone colourway. .

CANNONDALE JUDGE DOWNHILL/FREERIDE BIKE
Where? www.cannondale.com
How much? From £3,049/$5,569/€4,499
Available in three models, this awesome bike has state-of-the-art suspension and super-sporty aesthetic. The 6061 twin triangle mainframe has gone through over a hundred fatigue, impact and strength tests to ensure that it's as durable and high-performing as can be. The Judge is for serious mountain-biking enthusiasts who like to test their cycles to the limits.

Camera

Leica MP

Leica
MP

Where?
www.leica-camera.com •
Various outlets worldwide
How much?
£1,850/$3,258/€2,689

The digital age is upon us, with pundits predicting that film will soon be a thing of the past. Leica aficionados beg to differ, believing that these are the only cameras worth hanging round your neck, thanks to an unusually quiet shutter release, a commanding ability to take excellent pictures in even the gloomiest of light and, of course, handsome good looks. With a Leica you must wind the film on yourself and learn how to use a rangefinder – a separate viewfinder and focusing device. All these niggling idiosyncrasies are part of the reason why Leicas are so well-loved.

The German company has been making cameras since 1925 and actually invented 35-mm photography. Each camera has a number stamped on the top plate, and records show when it would have been made and how many were produced that year. Leicas entered photography mythology when Henri Cartier-Bresson, who was never seen without his Leica, buried his camera when he thought he was going to be captured during the Second World War.

The MP was first launched in 1956, and models from the 1950s and 1960s are now highly collectable. It was cleverly relaunched in 2003, something that provided a much-needed boost for Leica sales, as the company went on to sell more cameras than it had since 1968.

The MP model is still made by hand and, of course, includes a Leica lens – said to be the best. There is even an 'à la carte' service that allows Leica lovers to custom-build their camera; choices include Hermès calfskin.

And unlike digital cameras, many of which come and go in a flash, the Leica is easy to repair – indeed the company guarantees that new owners will be able to get hold of parts for their camera for at least 30 years after purchasing, something refreshing in a disposable consumer culture such as ours. No wonder people like Leica a lot.

PANASONIC LUMIX
Where? www.panasonic.com
How much? From £130/$229/€189
At the time of writing, this is one of the most reliable – not to say most reasonably priced – digital cameras. Some models include an ingenious anti-camera-shake system (as cameras get smaller, results get more shaky) and all have a Leica lens.

LOMO
Where? www.lomography.com
How much? £17/$30/€25
This cult Russian camera comes with a simple philosophy: 'Don't think, shoot.' The contemporary idea behind these cheap cameras, originally made as a mass-produced product during the Soviet era, is to take as many pictures as possible. The often imperfect and unpredictable results mean users can have a piece of art on their hands – even the kind of photograph it would take other photographers days to set up. Alternatively they could have a blurred mess. Either way, it's experimental.

Classic car

Aston Martin DB5

Aston Martin DB5

Where?
www.astonmartin.com •
www.collectorcartraderonline.com •
Classic car dealers
How much?
Price varies according to dealer

Cars have become one of the most pioneering and designed objects of the modern age, and are now among the most state-of-the-art, technologically exciting purchases you can make. But nothing carries quite the same kudos as a classic car. A symbol of style, class and utter refinement, a beautifully designed old-fashioned motor will garner raised eyebrows from across the street and – quite literally – stop traffic.

If there is one classic car that reigns high above the rest in terms of cool and good looks, it is a Bond car. The sleek and curvaceous Aston Martin DB5 is the one Sean Connery famously drove in *Goldfinger* – although his was equipped with machine guns, bulletproof shields, ejector seat and revolving licence plates. Founded in the UK by Lionel Martin and Robert Bamford in 1914, Aston Martin soon made a name for itself by making zippy racing cars, producing several for the French Grand Prix in the 1920s. In 1947, the company was bought by Sir David Brown – who gave his initials to the series to which the DB5 belongs. Only 886 of these cars were ever built, so you'll have to look long and hard if you want one, although you could, of course, opt for another model in the DB range. To this day, an exceptional level of workmanship goes into each Aston Martin produced. A classic, stylish and thoroughly refined choice.

JAGUAR E-TYPE

Where? www.jaguar.com • Classic car dealers • Henry Pearman of Eagle E-Types • 00 44 1825 830 966 • ww.eaglegb.com • E-Type Centre • 00 44 1827 373 247 • www.e-typecentre.co.uk
How much? From around £10,000/$17,800/ 14,500 for an average 2+2 Series 2 to £75,000/$130,000/€109,000 for an E-Type Roadster in good nick.
Also known as the E-type or XK-E, this magnificent car was designed by Malcolm Sayer, an aerodynamics engineer, and is distinctive due to its elongated bonnet and sleek, airplane-like structure. The fact that it could reach 150mph (241km/h) and cost half the price of its competitors when it was launched in 1963 caused a sensation. Sayer claimed it was the first car to be 'mathematically designed'. It was also the first sports car to be mass-produced – over 70,000 were built, which means it should be possible to track down a second-hand model within a few months. Then again, you can always opt for Jaguar's new take on the E-type, complete with a sleek, leather interior, control console with switches and baritone exhaust.

VOLVO P1800

Where? www.volvoclub.org.uk • volvo1800pictures.com • www.practicalclassics.co.uk
How much? From about £3,000/$5,293/€4,425
Yes it's a Volvo, the Swedish car manufacturers known for their angular and practical cars, but the P1800 also happens to be the company's coolest model. It shot to fame in the 1960s, after appearing as Roger Moore's preferred mode of transport in *The Saint*, and possesses a robust engine, an aerodynamic look and stylized fins. Less showy than a Bentley or Merc – a hip and affordable option indeed.

Golf driver

TaylorMade R7

Where?
www.taylormadegolf.com

How much?
Approximately £449/$795/€658

> '**G**olf is a game that is played on a five-inch course – the distance between your ears.'
>
> Bobby Jones, legendary golfer

A driver has been described as 'the club that separate contenders from the pretenders'. It is also the most expensive club in the bag, something that should also include a variety of woods, irons, a pitching wedge and a putter – golf rules allow a maximum of 14 clubs.

A driver is what a golfer uses to whack the ball when he or she tees-off – 'drive for show, putt for dough', so the saying goes – and male players in particular are obsessed with the length of their tee. The TaylorMade R7 is truly revolutionary. A driver that's currently most popular with professionals, as well as amateurs who can afford it, it is so prized, in fact, that many professional players use this brand for no financial reward.

The TaylorMade brand is renowned for its innovative use of new technology, and the R7 is no different, made up of a series of weights that can be adjusted using a special wrench to six different 'launch settings'. It is illegal to walk around a course adjusting the head of your clubs; instead, you set the driver to work around your weaknesses. When the R7 was first introduced a couple of years ago, it astounded the golf world. TaylorMade has since conceded that the R7 has a 95 per cent satisfaction rating and quite rightly describe it as 'the most highly awarded driver in the world'.

The company was started in Illinois in 1979 after the founder, Gary Adams, discovered balls struck by metal drivers travelled much further than those struck by traditional woods. Other brands worth buying for your bag include Titleist and Ping.

TaylorMade R7

CALLAWAY ERC FUSION
Where? www.callawaygolf.com
How much? From £249/$441/€365
The number-one selling brand in the United States (TaylorMade is number two), this driver is a mix of titanium and carbon, excellent for power and precision.

CLEVELAND LAUNCHER
Where? www.clevelandgolf.com
How much? From £83/$150/€116
A model with a big titanium head, this is the perfect driver for those with a high handicap.

Scooter

Vespa GTS250

Piaggio GTS250

Where?
www.vespa.com

How much?
Approximately £3,249/$5,750/€4,762

Vepsa is Italian for 'wasp' – and if you've ever heard one of these scooters zipping down a street, you'll know why. The vehicle was invented by Rinaldo Piaggio as the perfect cheap vehicle to get Italy moving again in the postwar period. He instructed his designers to create a scooter that was suitable for both men and women, could take a passenger and wouldn't get clothes dirty – crucial for fashion-conscious Italians.

The first Vespa was introduced in Italy in 1946 and was an immediate success, since it proved so skilled at dodging the country's bomb-scarred roads. Since then, Vespa has sold more than 16 million scooters worldwide and notable models include the LX, made famous by Audrey Hepburn in the movie *Roman Holiday*, and the ET2, which arrived on the scene in 1996 and helped invigorate sales in urban areas (this is the model Gwyneth Paltrow rides).

The GTS250 is the latest and most powerful Vespa yet and is an updated version of the GS (the Grand Sport), a model that is on permanent display at the Museum of Modern Art in New York. The GTS250 has Vespa's trademark rounded body and a top speed of 76mph (122 km/h) – it is so fast, in fact, that you'll need a motorcycle licence to ride it in the UK. Design features include a bar-mounted headlight and fold-down chrome rear rack headlight, plenty of underseat storage and a glove compartment.

Scooters have had a renaissance over the last few years, as commuters realize that they offer the quickest way of getting around increasingly congested cities. The updated features of the Vespa make it appealing to both sexes – men love the chrome-ringed instrument panel that looks like it belongs to an Italian sports car, while women wax lyrical about the 'curry rack' which is designed for hanging takeaways – or handbags.

PIAGGIO ZIP
Where? www.piaggio.com
How much? From £1,199/$2,122/€1,757
A ubiquitous sight on London's roads, this is the perfect urban model – cheap and easy to get around.

LAMBRETTA LD150
Where? Various specialist vintage dealers, including www.supersonicscooters.com and www.lambretta.co.uk
How much? Around £1,750/$3,097/€2,565
Lambretta was the main competition for Vepsa in the 1950s and 1960s. This model has two separate seats and is capable of 52mph (84km/h). It is still popular, although production ceased in the 1970s.

Skis

K2

Where?
www.k2skis.com •
Snow and Rock • www.snowandrock.com
How much?
From £299/$527/€441

K2 Appache skis

Rock paintings depict hunters skiing over 5,000 years ago and the Swedish army trained on skis in the 18th century, but the first skis resembling those we know today were invented in Norway in the 19th century. In 1928, the first aluminium ski was produced in France. Today, skis are shorter, wider and curvier than ever, with a greater variety of styles for varying levels of skill, though it's important you pick skis to suit your needs whether you're off for a week of on-piste skiing or a season of extreme off-piste endeavour. When it comes to skis, size and shape count. While jackets, salopettes and glasses are all of vital importance, the true skier knows that a good-quality pair of skis is paramount. It's not about simply buying the most expensive pair, but the ones that best suit your requirements. K2 is a fine Canadian brand that has devised skis for the expert skier. The Apache range provides particularly impressive specimens that can be used in any conditions and on any terrain, due to their expert construction from a material called Titan Metal Laminate.

VOLKL

Where? www.voelkl.com • Ellis Brigham, 3–11 Southampton Street, London, WC2 • 00 44 207 395 1010 • www.ellisbrigham.com
How much? From £500/$881/€738
This German brand offers a wide selection of skis, including the Unlimited range, which combines optimum ski width with the right amount of side cut and can be adapted to every ski style and level. In other words, this is a great all-rounder. Volkl's skis are also equipped with 'Double Grip' LT design and a corresponding absorption system.

ROSSIGNOL

Where? www.rossignol.com • Snow and Rock (see above)
How much? From £299/$530/€440
An excellent brand with a wide range of skis, particularly for women. The Bandit B4 is good for free-riding while the Open is excellent for those one-week-a-year skiers who want control and carving power.

Tennis racquet

Babolat Pure Drive

Where?
www.babolat.com •
www.tennis-warehouse.com •
Good sports shops worldwide

How much?
£100/$179/€148

Tennis dates back to the Tudor period, but the racquet has progressed greatly since then. Back in 1900, lawn tennis was big and racquets were small and loosely strung with grooved handles. In the 1920s, frames were made from solid ash and strung with piano wire. By the 1950s, metal was also being used to make frames, and by the 1980s, graphite racquets reigned supreme. Today, tennis racquets are generally lighter, with larger heads that improve control and speed. But what's the best of them all? While technology is constantly moving forward, Babolat's Pure Drive is currently considered one of the best racquets you can buy. Babolat has over 125 years experience at making top-notch designs. The 'Woofer' system generates power, since inside the frame are four symmetrical pulleys that contract on contact. The ball stays on the strings a split second longer – or so it feels – then bounces off with extra force. That's probably why Andy Roddick uses this brand for his record-breaking 155mph (250km/h) serve.

Babolat Pure Drive

WILSON NCODE NTOUR
Where? www.bellracquetsports.com
How much? £100/$179/€148
This lightweight frame is used by Lindsay Davenport. Gaps in the graphite frame are filled with silicone, which results in less vibration, more control and is less likely to cause tennis elbow. Wilson also claim this racquet is twice as strong and stable as a normal racquet and up to 22 per cent more powerful than an ordinary graphite frame. The head is larger than usual and good for intermediate players who still want some pop from the racquet, while gaining control. For keen amateurs, Wilson is also the chicest brand.

PRINCE O3 SILVER
Where? www.princetennis.com • www.racket-sport.com
How much? £160/$260/€234
Large 'O' ports around the frame give this racquet extra spring, which means it moves through the air more quickly, making it easier to return those smashes. Those 'O's also create a bigger sweet spot (the area on the strings that produces the best combination of feel and power), so it takes minimal energy to hit the ball and the player is able to focus on technique.